CANADIAN FLY FISHING

Hot Spots & Essentials

CANADIAN FLY FISHING
Hot Spots & Essentials

Duane S. Radford

PARTNERS
PUBLISHING

LONE
PINE

Co-published by Partners Publishing and Lone Pine Media Productions (B.C.) Ltd.

Distributed by: Canada Book Distributors - Booklogic
11414-119 Street
Edmonton, AB   T5G 2X6   Canada
Tel: 1-800-661-9017

Canadian Cataloguing in Publication Data
Radford, Duane, 1946–, author
  Canadian fly fishing hot spots and essentials / Duane S. Radford.
Includes bibliographical references.

Partners Publishing
ISBN 978-1-77213-040-9 (paperback)
ISBN 978-1-77213-041-6 (epub)

Lone Pine Media Productions
ISBN 978-1-55105-957-0 (paperback)
ISBN 978-1-55105-958-7 (epub)

1. Fly fishing—Canada—Guidebooks. 2. Fly fishing—Canada. I. Title.
SH456.R33 2017   799.12'40971   C2017-900963-X

Project Editor: Sheila Cooke
Production Manager: Leslie Hung
Layout and Production: Tamara Hartson
Cover Design: Gregory Brown

Photos: All photos are copyright Duane Radford except: p. 45 Greg Buck; p. 49 James O'Farrell; pp. 64, 82, 143 Amelia Jensen; p. 66 Trevor Nowak; pp. 79, 104, 105, 107, 108, 109, 110b Jeff Smith; p. 127 Nick Didlick; p. 136a&b Alberta Fish and Wildlife; pp. 138, 139a Mark Christiansen; pp. 139b, 140a Don Anderson; p. 141 Neil Waugh; p. 145a&b Fred Noddin; p. 166 Claude Bernard; p. 215b Craig Blackie.

We acknowledge the financial support of the Government of Canada.

Funded by the Government of Canada
Financé par le gouvernement du Canada | Canadä

Dedication

I'd like to dedicate this book to members of my family who have provided me so much support and encouragement over the years in my outdoor adventures. We've enjoyed some of the best days of our lives at various fish camps and backcountry hideaways across this great nation of ours. I can't say enough about my wife, Adrienne, with whom I've spent many wonderful days on the water. Adrienne has become quite a fly fisher in her own right and has accompanied me on numerous fishing trips. To my daughter, Jennifer, I'll always remember the days we spent hiking and fishing in southern Alberta, and especially the memorable time we hiked along the magnificent Carthew Lakes Trail in Waterton Lakes National Park. To my son, Myles, I knew you'd turn out to be a fine outdoorsman after we hiked into Crypt Lake in Waterton Lakes National Park—one of Canada's top backcountry adventures—when you didn't blink as we hugged a cliff with a thousand foot drop-off along a precipice at one spot on the challenging trail.

Table of Contents

Acknowledgements

This book would not have been possible without the support of several Canadian tourism departments that facilitated and often hosted trips to various fishing lodges and municipal centres. In this regard, I'd like to express my thanks and appreciation to Elora and Fergus Tourism, Northwest Territories Tourism & Parks, Nunavut Tourism, Newfoundland and Labrador Tourism, Saskatchewan Tourism, Tourism British Columbia, Tourism New Brunswick, Travel Alberta and Yukon Tourism and Culture.

I'm indebted to the guides who shared their knowledge and experience on fly fishing tips and techniques for local waters, information that has made me a better fly fisher. Upon reflection, I've been truly blessed to have been able to patch up with a wonderful line-up of so many top-notch Canadian fishing guides: Bill Abercrombie, John Avery, Pat Babcock, Donald Beek, Vic Bergman, Garrett Braun, Greg Buck, Orville Caddy, Aaron Caldwell, Clint Caldwell, Ron Chambers, Jamey Cloete, Lorne Currie, Brian Dack, Nick Didlick, Dan Drummond, Brad Eliason, Jan-Eric (Jack) Elofsson, Tony Gellings, Allan Hansen, John Huff, Wade Istchenko, Dave Jensen, Kelly Kizan, Ray Kohlruss, Dustin Kovacvich, Lonny LaRoque, Ryan MacDonald, Mike Mailey, Dan Miguel, C. Perry Munro, Larry Nagy, Trevor Nowak, James & David O'Farrell, John Oracz, Don Pike, Dennis Pilgrim, Keith Rae, Sky Richard, Darcy Richardson, Paul Samycia, Thomas Staub, Joe Toutsaint, Russell Trand, Alexis Thuillier, Ricky Wagner, Barry White and Larry Willet. Fishing guides generally know where to find fish, and some are indeed experts in this regard; Vic Bergman, Thomas Staub and Russell Trand have a seemingly uncanny knowledge where fish are holed up. Barry White is an expert fly caster who can coach neophytes to become better fly fishers, while guides Darcy Richardson and John Avery are fly fishing technical gurus bar none.

I'd like to thank Mike Shickler for drafting the map of Canada used in the Introduction of this book.

Last, but not least, I want to acknowledge several book, magazine and newspaper editors who've improved my writing since I started outdoor and travel writing in 1995: Stacey Aaronson, Camille Atebe, Faye Boer, Nicholle Carrière, Kim Crawford, Tracey Ellis, Gord Follett, George Gruenefeld, Dave Hughes, Michelle Manson, Chris Marshall, Teri Mason, Rob Miskosky, Warren Perley, Wendy Pirk, Steve Probosco, Randy Roszell, Bob Sexton, John Shewey, Doug Smith, Patrick Walsh, David Webb, Annabelle Wright, Janet Vleig, Al Voth and Mark Yelic.

I'd also like to thank Sheila Cooke, who edited this book, for her candour, impeccable attention to detail and overall editorial insight.

There's a saying that every writer needs a good editor; I very much appreciate the comments and constructive criticism these editors have provided.

Foreword

Let me get this out of the way first: you probably shouldn't read this book if you're prone to fly fishing envy. That's because you, like me, are going to read about a whole bunch of places you want to fish, but haven't.

The good news, though, is that Duane Radford has been doing the advance scouting of these places on our behalf for decades. So when we follow in his fly fishing footsteps, we'll find that he's done much of the legwork for us. We'll know when to go, what flies and tackle to take and how to best use that tackle when we get there.

And just look at the list of Canadian fishing Meccas he talks about in this book. Always dreamed of an Arctic char from the Tree River? There's a wealth of information about that mystical place in here, and likely more information about fly fishing the Yukon and Northwest Territories than you'll find anywhere else.

What about steelhead or coho on the west coast, or giant pike on your fly rod? If you want to find out when, where and how, it's in this book. Or how about the lowly gold-eye and mountain whitefish? They're here too, and you might find that the best fishing for them is just beyond your backyard.

Duane knows fish both as a fisherman and as a scientist. His passion and enthusiasm for fly fishing is supported and verified by his training and experience in fisheries biology and fisheries management, and this gives exceptional credibility to his observations and opinions.

I haven't yet fished with Duane, and that's my loss. But I've got this book, and that's the next best thing. So, on second thought, maybe you *should* read this book, for if you take some of Duane's advice on technique and lean on his experience to guide you to a dream trip in a magical destination, you might just be the one dispensing the fly fishing envy.

–Jim McLennan, author of *Blue Ribbon Bow* and *Trout Streams of Alberta*

Introduction

*Our tradition is that of the first man who sneaked away to
the creek when the tribe did not really need fish.*
—Roderick Haig-Brown, *A River Never Sleeps*, 1946

Fifteen years ago I couldn't have written this book about fly fishing Canada's hot spots. Back then I didn't have the skills and knowledge to fly fish for the wide range of species I've caught since 2000 across Canada, from the Atlantic to the Pacific to the Arctic oceans. It's been quite a ride, and I've had many hair-raising trips most anglers could only dream about experiencing. Several jet boat rides on Yukon's Kathleen River still bring chills to my spine, much like the first time I stepped off a Turbo Otter on the banks of Nunavut's

famed Tree River. Along the way, I've had to do a lot of research to determine what kind of fly fishing tackle and paraphernalia I should pack on the assortment of nationwide fly fishing junkets I've experienced.

This book is loaded with fly fishing tips, from the basics of fly fishing, to how to gear up for a fly fishing trip, to how to read and fly fish a trout stream. There are tips on how to fly fish pocket water, how to fish dry flies and wet flies, nymphs and steamers; how to fly fish from drift boats and rubber rafts, as well as information about the plethora of

Fly fishing for Atlantic salmon on the Miramichi River, New Brunswick.

boats used for fly fishing in Canada. There's a section on the importance of water temperature to fly fishers and why you should never leave home without a pocket thermometer. There is information on how to fly fish for some of Canada's unpublicized fish such as goldeye, northern pike, mountain whitefish, Arctic grayling and lake trout, and how to land Mr. Big.

For the uninitiated, here you will find information on fly fishing for trophy lake trout, Arctic char and monster northern pike in Canada's high Arctic, where fish are measured in feet, not inches, as well as the kind of fly fishing gear you need to land a 35-pound behemoth. I've included hatch information for the early, mid and late season North of 60, that wild expanse of wilderness north of the 60th parallel—the first time such information has been published. There are virtually no fly shops in Canada's north; consequently, you'd better

be prepared before you leave home and have a well-stocked fly box. Then there are Arctic grayling, the quintessential fly fishermen's dream fish, an absolute delight on a light-weight fly rod; what kind of go-to flies should you buy? Read on to find out.

I've taken marble-backed brook trout in the wilds of Labrador. I've landed Atlantic salmon in the fabled Miramichi River in New Brunswick, and trophy rainbows and brown trout in Alberta's world-renowned Bow River. I've had the good fortune to have fly fished Quebec's idyllic Kenauk Reserve several times for rainbows and brook trout, and stayed in romantic backcountry cabins by Lac Colins and Lake Taunton. I've enjoyed time on Ontario's Grand River, a fisheries success story in the making. I've spent many days on some of the best fly fishing waters in British Columbia. I've broken a lot of new ground with the help of some great fishing guides.

I'm now confident I've got a story to tell that will be invaluable to the itinerant fly fisher.

Canada is blessed with some outstanding fly fishing waters; unfortunately, much of it has never been publicized. Nor has much information been publicized on how to fly fish many of these hot spots, useful knowledge that can be used elsewhere. There's nothing quite like fly fishing on Yukon's top stream for rainbow trout: the Kathleen River, one of the gems in Canadian fly fishing. There are several dream float trips in southwestern Alberta that should be on every fly fisher's bucket list for rainbow trout, brown trout, cutthroat trout, bull trout and mountain whitefish. Then there's the Elk River in British Columbia, one of Canada's top streams for cutthroat trout.

Canada boasts many great lodges, only a fraction of which are featured in this book. Some lodges have so much magic that one trip is just not enough. I've been back to some, such as the Dalton Trail Lodge in Yukon, six times, and I've yet to be satisfied. Then there's Plummer's Tree River Lodge in Nunavut. The Tree River boasts the world record Arctic char—it's like a beautiful, irresistible woman whose charm never diminishes, so it was imperative for me to make a second trip to this most challenging river. A photo of my son, Myles, with a magnificent Arctic char graces the title page of this book and was taken during the second trip I made to this wild river.

A note about this guide: officially, measurements are in metric in Canada, not imperial units, but because anglers normally use the units of pounds, inches and feet when they're sizing their catch and measuring water depth, generally no metric equivalents will be cited in this book when referring to the size of fish or the depth of water.

Enjoy a dream float trip on the Upper Castle River, Alberta.

Chapter 1

Fly Fishing Fundamentals: The Gear

My biggest worry is that when I am dead and gone, my wife will sell my fishing gear for what I said I paid for it.

—Koos Brandt

Tackle Basics

There are several options you should consider relative to the type of fly fishing you want to pursue and your budget. If you're on a budget, you can purchase a basic, beginner fly package kit, which includes a versatile 6-weight graphite fly rod, fly reel, floating line, backing for the fly line and a leader. A fly fishing vest is also a good investment to hold fly boxes, extra reels and spools and various other fly fishing accessories.

Fly Rods

The most important piece of fly fishing equipment is the fly rod. While fly rods come in bamboo, fibreglass and graphite, I suggest you purchase a graphite rod; graphite rods are a pleasure to cast. Most modern rods are made of graphite and come with a cork grip. They range in length from 7 1/2 to 10 feet; 9 feet is the most common.

Fly rod weights range from 1 to 14. The rod weight should be geared to the size of

Tackle basics include a fly rod, reel, line, leader and fly patterns.

your quarry, with a size 2–4 rod being suitable for small to medium-sized trout and Arctic grayling, on up to an 8-weight (or greater) rod for really large fish. Many anglers opt for 5- or 6-weight rods, which are a good all-around choice for small to medium fish.

Fly rods also have action ratings: extra fast, fast, moderate (medium) and slow. The faster the action, the longer the cast. Slow actions are best suited for short casts. Medium action is most suitable for the widest range of conditions. Beginners generally find fly rods with fast or moderate actions the easiest to cast.

Fly Reels

You can purchase an extra spool with most fly reels: one for a floating line and the other for a sinking line, or sink tip line. Most reels come with a disc drag system (to play fish), which is a good feature to protect a light tippet from hard charging, large fish. Fly reels range widely in price. Economical reels use a click or pawl drag system that employs a spring on a gear system to slow down the reel when a fish is running with your line.

Small-, medium- or large-arbour reels should be selected depending on the type of fly fishing you're into, with large-arbour reels being best for large fish such as big lake trout and pike, and small- and medium-arbour reels suitable for small- to medium-size fish. Large-arbour reels have the best rates of retrieve.

An 8-weight rod with a large-arbour reel is necessary for large fish.

Match the rod weight and dry fly line weight.

Fly Line

A fly line has the difficult job of transporting the fly to the fish; it's another important component to think about when gearing up. Line weights run from 1 to 12 and are measured in grains: 1 is the lightest (60 grains); 12 is the heaviest (380 grains). The weight of the fly line should be matched with the rod weight for a proper cast. The stronger the wind and the heavier the fly, the heavier the line needs to be to cast the fly effectively. Line weights in the 2–4 range are light duty for small trout; they're tough to cast in a stiff breeze and don't handle flies larger than size 14 very well. Line weights 5–7 are general purpose. They'll handle most of the flies used for trout and also have enough weight to take wind better than the lighter lines. Line weights 8–10 are commonly used for large fish and have the necessary weight to carry big flies long distances.

Fly lines come with different tapers: double taper and weight forward are the most common. Weight forward lines have most of the weight positioned in the forward portion of the fly line. They have a "WF" designation on the box. This design produces a line that's easy to cast and also handles wind fairly well. It's the best line for beginners to cast and the one most often used in beginner's kits. Double taper lines are tapered at both ends of the line and are designated "DT" on the line box. They're generally for more delicate casts. They don't cast as far as weight forward lines and can be troublesome in the wind.

Fly lines also come in three basic types: floating, sinking and sink tip. They're labelled "F" for floating, "S" for sinking and "F/S" for floating/sinking tip. Floating lines are generally used for fishing with dry flies, but they may also be employed for fishing with nymphs and streamers in certain situations. Sinking lines (and those with sink tips) are used for fishing with nymphs, wet flies and streamers. Sink tip lines are generally used for casting streamers in relatively shallow water with moderate currents. Full sink lines are for fishing in deep water and/or swift currents.

Line manufacturers put all these weights and other designations on the line box. A "WF5F/S" designation means it is a 5-weight line with a weight forward taper, floating with a sinking tip.

Leaders, Tippets and Backing

A leader is a tapered length of monofilament line that is used to attach a fly to the fly line. Leaders are tapered (for ease of casting) to a thin tippet (of a particular diameter and length) at the end of the leader. The fat end is tied to the fly line, usually with a nail knot. The tippet is where you tie your fly. Most leaders range in length from 7 1/2 to 9 feet, up to 12 feet; a 9-foot tapered leader is a good all-around length. Extra tippet material can be added to a leader to replace lost tippet material or to use a different size of fly—tie the tippet to the end of the tapered leader using a double surgeon's knot. It's made of the same material as the leader.

Tippets come in different diameters from 8X down to 1X. Generally, 1X is for big, heavy flies; 2X is for flies size 8–10; 3X is for flies size 10–12; 4X is for flies size 12–14; etc. The larger the "X" on a numbered tippet, the smaller the tippet weight. If you've selected a size 12 dry fly, use the "4 Rule" to select a tippet size: divide the size of the fly hook, 12, by 4, which equals 3, so the appropriate tippet weight would be 3X. Normally, tippets are cut about 3 feet in length. They'll break instead of the more expensive tapered leaders and fly line should you get snagged.

Backing is thin Dacron (generally) line that's attached between the reel and the fly line. It provides extra line to fight large fish and minimizes fly line memory. Backing is tied onto the fly line with an Albright knot.

Flies

Most avid fly fishers have a large selection of four basic categories of fly patterns—dry

The objective of fly fishing is to cast a fly pattern that imitates food that fish eat.

There's been an explosion in fly fishing products over the past few years.

flies, wet flies, nymphs and streamers—to deal with different circumstances. Nymphs, wet flies and streamers are all fished below the surface. Dry flies are fished on the surface. A key difference between nymphs and wet flies is the absence of a soft hackle on the thorax of nymphs.

Flies come in numbered sizes 1 to 32, with small numbers representing large hooks and the large numbers representing small hooks. A size 24 fly is so small it's hard to see and even harder to tie onto a tippet without the aid of a magnifying glass; you can imagine how hard it is to spot a fly of this size on the water. However, this changes when you move past 1 the other way. Now, the larger the number, the larger the hook. This change is differentiated by adding a zero behind the larger hook size—for example, 1/0, which is bigger than a 1, followed by a 2/0, which is even bigger. This system gives you the very small size 32 to the huge 20/0.

Gearing Up for a Fly Fishing Trip

This is but a brief summary of what you'll need to gear up for fly fishing trips in Canada. The choice of rod weights, actions, reels and lines is fairly complicated; however, unless you get it right, you'll find fly casting very frustrating. If you match the rod weight, action, reel and lines, casting is much easier.

Fly fishing newbies might want to purchase a starter fly fishing package: a matching fly rod, reel and line suitable for the type of fly fishing they have in mind. If one purchases a 6-weight fly rod, select a 6-weight fly line (floating, sink tip and full sink) to match, with a medium- or large-arbour reel, for example. If you're after big pike, an 8-weight, medium-action fly rod with an 8-weight, sink tip fly line and a large-arbour reel would be my recommendation to cast large streamers and play large fish.

I've opted for three basic fly rod weights: a 4-weight for small streams and fish, a 6-weight for medium to large rivers and fish and an 8-weight for large streams and fish. I have a selection of floating, sink tip and full sink lines with medium- and large-arbour reels for each rod weight. My 4-weight rods are a joy to cast and make fly casting virtually effortless. My 6-weight rod is great for punching flies over a distance. My 8-weight, medium-action rods also cast well and are capable of landing 35-pound or larger fish.

There's no universal rule that dictates the appropriate size of fly when fly fishing or whether a dry fly, nymph or streamer would work best; it all depends on the circumstances. If there's an insect hatch, it's best to match the hatch with an appropriate fly pattern and size. Under some circumstances, going a size or two larger doesn't hurt and may actually lead to more rises. On waters that are heavily fished, however, trout can become shy of large flies, and it's often better to use a size 14–16 or smaller.

There's lots of other useful fly fishing gear:

- fly boxes of various sizes to store different patterns

- forceps to dislodge stuck hooks

- leader clippers to trim tag lines

- compounds to clean and condition fly lines and to ease casting

- strike indicators for nymphing

- dry fly dressing to keep flies buoyant

- a fly vest to store these gadgets

- a landing net

- breathable waders

- anti-slip felt-soled wading boots

- gravel guards that keep sand and gravel out of wading boots are a good buy for waders that don't have these features

- for still-water anglers, water craft round out the equipment list: a belly boat, pontoon boat, canoe or car top boat, etc., to get around on the water.

Fly fishing vests remain popular items.

If you're just getting into fly fishing, I suggest you develop an equipment checklist so you are properly equipped and don't leave anything at home.

If you've never fly fished, it's a good idea to get some lessons on fly casting. It's not hard to learn but takes some practice before you become proficient at making casts with pinpoint accuracy. You could sign up for a fly casting course, or seek out a fly casting mentor to get some lessons. You could also learn by doing and go on a guided fly fishing trip where the guide can teach you how to cast at the same time as you're actually fishing. Canada is blessed with many outstanding fly fishing guides, all a phone call away. My suggestion if you're going the guided route is to book a walk-and-wade trip first, rather than a trip with a drift boat or rubber raft; do those trips later when you've got your casting down pat.

Fly fishing is a catharsis for your everyday worries. There's something about the rhythm of casting that's also very relaxing. And just making a good cast is a reward in itself even if you don't get a strike.

Guard socks (below) fit over top of wading boots to act as gravel guards; a landing net (right) is a must-have accessory.

Canadian Fly Fishing Boats

There's a plethora of boats that a fly angler will encounter across Canada that will present challenges because fly fishing line tends to get caught up on all manner of things, and each boat is different, so casting styles must be flexible.

Ever heard of a Gander River boat? Me neither, until I booked a trip at Awesome Lake Lodge in the Labrador wilderness. What are they like on the water for fly fishing?

What about Mackenzie-style drift boats and inflatable rubber rafts—self draining and otherwise, with or without a bow and/ or stern leg brace? Do you know how to cast from these water craft in a swift, free-stone western river where pinpoint casts are the norm and casting options often fleeting at best? What are the pros and cons of drift boats vs. rubber rafts?

On to lakes—what kind of outboards should you be prepared to fish from on large lakes where trophy lake trout and northern pike might be your quarry? What are some of the casting hazards associated with outboard boats that should be a red flag to fly fishers?

For the dedicated fly fisher, I'd suggest preparing for various contingencies because you're bound to run into Gander River boats, Mackenzie-style drift boats, inflatable rafts, an array of outboard motorboats, as well as the quintessential Canadian freighter canoe somewhere along the way.

Canadian fly fishers must be able to cast from a plethora of different boat styles.

Gander River boats are often used in Newfoundland and Labrador.

Gander River Boats

Gander River boats are standard fare at many fish camps in Newfoundland and Labrador. These iconic boats were originally used to navigate the Gander River in Newfoundland, ferrying outfitters and their clients between fish camps on the river. The original boats were handcrafted of spruce, well built and very sturdy.

Today the boats are still handmade, mostly by guides along the Gander River. They are often a winter project—a new one is made each winter. Each one is unique. They are between 20 and 24 feet long, and they have a shallow draft and ride high on the water. They're also very stable; it's no problem to stand in them to cast, and trolling is a breeze. They have virtually no accoutrements to get snagged on, which is yet another nice feature.

What impressed me most aside from Gander River boats' stability was their storage capacity. The boats have all sorts of room for extra rod cases. The downside is that they don't have a very large enclosed storage area in the bow; consequently some gear may be open to the weather. Actually, some Gander River boats may not have any enclosed areas. Fly fishers should bring dry bags or waterproof packs to keep their gear dry because it has been known to rain 24/7 at Newfoundland and Labrador fish camps. Another requirement when using these craft is footwear with good grips, which are essential when the decks are wet.

Mackenzie-style Drift Boats

Some of my best days on the water have been spent in Mackenzie-style drift boats on large freestone rivers in western Canada's foothills and mountains. These craft were designed for fly fishing and are everywhere on streams such as Alberta's famed Bow River. They're extremely stable, can handle white water and rarely ship any water. But even though drift boats have a shallow draft, they can get hung up on bars

Mackenzie-style drift boats are used on many large rivers in Alberta and British Columbia.

in shallow water and can be brutes to get unstuck. They're really the Cadillac of fly fishing boats as long as there's enough water to keep them buoyant. These boats have storage compartments up front and at the back of the boat, as well as under the guide's seat, where you stow your day gear. There is room on the side of a drift boat for rod cases.

The oarsman or guide sits in the middle of the boat, facing downstream, and rows against the current to slow the boat down or steers as necessary. Experienced guides are expert at angling drift boats towards the best lairs to aid fly casting. There are comfortable seats fore and aft for the sports. In front of each seat is a leg brace. The sport up front must have both legs wedged into the brace at all times when standing up. The sport in the back must have at least one leg, but not necessarily both, wedged in the brace at all times. These are basic safety precautions to avoid spills.

The drill is generally to cast downstream, although side casts are fairly common,

especially for the sport in the stern. Because streams in the foothills and mountains can be fairly swift, the downside is that on many occasions the sports will only be able to make one cast into promising holding water. You must be able to cast well, especially when dry fly fishing, to enjoy time spent in Mackenzie-style drift boats and not get frustrated. While straight-line casts are the norm, it's wise to be adept at roll casts, reach casts, side casts and chop casts (see page 28). Gear up with belted chest waders, have a day pack with rain gear, and be prepared for a fair measure of walk-and-wade fishing, as is also the case when fishing from inflatable rafts.

The Mackenzie-style drift boat has high gunwales; you'll have to lift your legs over the gunwales to get in and out. Always keep one hand on the gunwale to balance yourself when you are getting in or out—you don't want to slip and break your rod or injure yourself. Also keep your feet and hands free of the rope attached to the lead anchor in the stern to avoid accidents.

Inflatable Rafts

Inflatable rafts are the ticket for those streams that are troublesome to float in Mackenzie-style drift boats, which tend to get hung up on bars in shallow water, and on rivers with lots of rock outcrops or ledges, which are downright dangerous to navigate in a drift boat. While shallow bars can also be a challenge for inflatable rafts, at least the rafts don't weigh as much as drift boats and can be muscled into floatable water when they come aground. And while it is inadvisable to try to run outcrops with a significant drop off with a drift boat because it will almost certainly capsize, a raft can handle most outcrops with ease and simply snake their way over such obstacles. An additional advantage of rafts is that they don't require formal boat ramps and can be slid into and taken out of a stream in rugged places.

Although a raft may ship some water, it won't sink and will rarely tip over—the better rafts are even self-draining. A downside of rafts is they don't have a lot of storage space (especially out of the weather), so keep your gear to a minimum. The trick getting in and out is to simply sit on the gunwale and swing your body into the raft and onto a seat, and vice versa to disembark—no problem. Don't try to stand on the rubber sides of a raft because chances are you'll end up losing your balance. Rafts come with comfortable seats that swivel. The better quality rafts feature a bow/stern

This is a modern rubber raft with an aluminum floor.

Inflatable rubber rafts are commonly used on inaccesible streams for fly fishing.

leg brace, which certainly beats casting while sitting down and makes it much easier for the sports to see what lies ahead.

Most guides will steer the raft at an angle so that both sports can see their target. Cast your fly precisely; you'll likely have only one good chance for a hook-up. Because you generally have to sit when fishing from a raft, just swivel the seat to get pointed in the right direction and then make a straight-line or side cast. When casting while sitting down, the trick is to lower your casting trajectory to stay on target; nonetheless, this method is a challenge for newbie fly fishers who are used to standing up when casting.

Outboard Motorboats

Boats with large outboard motors are typically used at most fishing lodges in Canada's north because they are good work boats that travel fast and can handle rough water.

Lodges that cater to pike fly fishers may have customized Jon boats with casting platforms that are ideal to target pike in shallow water. Other lodges that specialize in pike fishing may have Lund Alaskans with carpeted decks and spacious storage bins to keep the deck free of obstacles and minimize snags. I'm sold on the 16-foot Lund Alaskans with 40-horsepower outboard motors and spacious, wide open floors, lots of storage capacity and padded, swivel pedestal seats for pike fishing. These boats are very stable and are excellent to fly fish from.

Other lodges on some of Canada's largest lakes feature 18-foot Lund Alaskans with 30-horsepower outboards. Most of these boats have limited storage capacity, and what little is available is generally used to store gear for shore lunches, spare gas tanks and the like. Bring a waterproof storage container for your fly fishing gear and camera. Also dress for the weather because it can be downright chilly on a large, northern lake even in the middle of summer.

Technically, a 12- or 14-foot long aluminum car top boat would also fit in the

Outboard motor boats are often used in Canada's North Country.

category of outboard motorboats and is on occasion used for fly fishing, often with an outboard motor for propulsion or perhaps an electric motor where gas motors are prohibited by law.

All outboard motorboats present some challenges for fly fishers who are pitching large streamers, which can be awkward to cast regardless of whether the fly fisher is using floating or sink tip lines. Streamers are often the fly of choice for pike and lake trout. The sport in the bow has the best position and can use roll casts, straight-line casts and Belgian casts at leisure. However, the fly fisher in the middle of the boat has a more limited number of casting options; furthermore, he has to avoid not only line tangles with his partner but also hitting the guide (in the stern) with his streamer. Whether you're in the bow or middle of the boat, you'll have to use the water to load your fly rod and then work a large streamer out towards the strike zone. It's no problem to troll streamers from an outboard motorboat, and about the only significant hazard is getting your fly line caught in the propeller.

A dry pack is a must-have item for boats with limited storage.

Freighter canoes are used on lakes where gas-powered motorboats are not allowed.

Freighter Canoes

Freighter canoes fitted with electric motors are the boat of choice on many lakes in Canada's national parks and present some unique challenges for fly fishers. Experienced boaters pack a spare electric motor and extra batteries because these boats are not easy to paddle on a lake. They have limited storage capacity, so keep your gear to a minimum, and be sure to dress well; otherwise you're going to be cold.

It's not difficult to troll streamers in a freighter canoe when using full sink lines, and about the only thing to watch out for would be propeller tangles. While you can stand up in a freighter canoe to cast if the lake is calm, most casting is done from a sitting position, generally tossing bead head nymphs or chironomids with a floating line equipped with a strike indicator. Newbies may have trouble casting chiron-

omids or nymphs if they don't know how to use the water to load the rod and work the fly out into the target zone. Also, fly fishers not used to casting from a sitting position often don't realize they simply have to change their casting trajectory to make things work.

Jet Boats

Jet boats are used to run swift, shallow rivers to get into fly fishing territory, and most sports do not actually fly fish while the boats are in motion. The only casting from a jet boat happens when it's anchored near a hot spot.

I've fly fished using jet boats on several large rivers in Alberta and Yukon, and I have been impressed with their versatility. They have a shallow draft, are stable and most have lots of storage capacity and are fairly easy to get in and out of without falling or tripping, which can be an issue when wearing chest waders. At times travelling in a jet boat can be downright exhilarating, but these boats require an experienced, knowledgeable operator at the helm.

Boston Whalers

Boston Whalers are commonly used at salmon fishing lodges on the west coast to troll streamers in search of coho salmon in particular. These high-end outboard motorboats are fine craft indeed. They are renowned for their stability and are very safe to fish from. They do not present any special challenges when trolling flies for salmon.

Not all lodges provide fishing guides; in such cases you'll be solo in your Boston Whaler and will require a valid Canadian Pleasure Craft Operator Card to be in compliance with the law. You also need to

Jet boats are used on large, turbulent rivers in northern Canada.

be prepared for foul weather when on the west coast, where rain is common. Rubber-soled shoes or boots are a must.

Now you know the skinny on fly fishing from various boats, whether it be casting or trolling—the good, the bad and the ugly!

Boston Whalers are used on the ocean to fly fish for coho salmon.

Chapter 2

Fly Fishing Fundamentals: The Technique

O, sir, doubt not that Angling is an art; is it not an art to deceive a trout with an artificial fly?

–Isaak Walton

Fly Casting

The basics of fly casting are of fundamental importance in order to cast with pinpoint accuracy and with a drag-free drift when stream fishing. If a fly is moving faster than the current, your chances of a hook-up, let alone a rise, are slim. Accurate casts and a drag-free drift are also important when casting nymphs, with or without a strike indicator, or streamers and wet flies.

Starting with the casting stance, if you are right-handed, put your left foot forward. Left-handed casters should do the opposite. Keep your shoulders straight, at right angles to the spot you're casting towards. The reason to keep your shoulders straight is to ensure you don't cause the fly line to curve when it is released. This is the routine casting stance for your basic straight-line cast. When power casting, right-handed

The power or handshake grip is recommended for fly casting.

fly fishers should put their right foot forward, then lean into the cast to lower their casting trajectory.

You can use one of two grips. The **power** or **handshake** grip has the caster's thumb on top of the cork grip on the handle of the fly rod. You can also use a **key grip**: imagine that you're holding a key in your hand, and put it over the cork grip. Your thumb will be on one side of the grip and your index finger on the other. Don't twist your hand or wrist while you cast, which will cause your fly to go awry. Your wrist should move back and forth in delivering the cast, not your arm, with your elbow being the fulcrum.

The most basic cast is called a straight-line cast. Other types of casts are specialty casts: roll casts, reach casts and chop casts or sidearm casts.

A **straight-line cast** is used to deliver a fly by casting the line in a straight direction towards your target. Start by stripping some line from the reel, and lay it at your feet or hold it in your left hand (if you're right-handed). Make a high back cast. Then accelerate the fly rod forward and throw a forward loop, keeping the tip of your rod in a horizontal plane as the rod itself moves in a vertical plane. Let your line go when your rod tip is straight out in front of you. Use only enough power to lay the line out straight. Use short strokes for short casts and long strokes for long casts. Don't overpower your forward cast or the line will fall in a pile at your feet. Keep slack line to a minimum; don't use any more line than necessary to reach your target.

You may have to make a few false casts to load the rod with enough line to reach your target. Again, to prevent loops and hooks, the tip of the rod should be on a horizontal plane at the same time that the length of the rod is on a vertical plane as you load your rod prior to casting. Otherwise, it will create a big loop, which will

A straight-line cast is the most basic of all casts.

cause the fly line to crash short of its target. Imagine keeping the rod tip parallel to the ceiling in a room as you stand beside a wall, keeping the fly rod moving parallel to that wall; do not hook it from side to side.

Try to minimize false casts: they're tiring and are not usually necessary except perhaps to dry off your fly. It's much easier to dope up a dry fly than to be forever making false casts to shake water from its dressing. For large flies such as streamers, use the water to load the fly rod rather than employing false casts.

If you're having trouble with your forward casting rhythm and/or your back cast, resort to an old trick: while holding the fly line in your left hand, swing both your right and left arms backwards and forwards in unison until you get your rhythm back.

Fly casting is something you don't forget, but anybody may have problems with their casting rhythm from time to time.

You can use a **roll cast** (or simply strip line from the reel) to get some line out before you make a straight-line cast. A roll cast is much like it sounds: get a firm grip on the handle of the fly rod, twist your wrist and roll (flick) your hand to pick up the fly line by pitching it forward, all in the same motion. The rod flex will pick up the slack line and propel it forward. Sometimes, you may have to use a few roll casts to get the casting distance you want. Practice roll casts whenever the opportunity arises; they're useful when fly fishing in tight quarters—in a boat or up against streamside vegetation—when you don't want to snag anything.

It takes practice to cast a fly; there's no substitute for experience.

Pause on your back cast so you don't get a trailing loop.

Bending the rod is the same as loading the rod; bending creates the forward and backward motion of the fly line. If you cast (release) your fly line when the tip of your rod is too far forward, your fly line will pile up in front of you.

Russell Trand, an old friend of mine (and former fishing guide) from Fernie, British Columbia, uses the mantra "pause, stop, mend" as a coaching technique when stream fishing: pause during your back cast; stop halfway to the horizon and let the fly drop; and mend by immediately looping the fly line upstream upon contact with the water so the fly floats drag free in the drift. This is actually called a **reach cast**; you don't have to mend if you're fishing still waters.

Barry White, Bow River Anglers fishing guide, has his own pet phrase: "Stab the sky! Hurl the hatchet!" on the back cast and forward motion, respectively.

Try to develop your own casting style. You don't necessarily need to stop your back cast at the 1 o'clock position and your forward cast at the 10 o'clock position, which are textbook recommendations.

Use a **double haul** to increase the speed of the fly line as you're false casting. Strip line while you are making a back cast, and feed line to the rod. Down is for speed. Up is for feeding line. Remember down/up when doing the double haul.

Use a **chop cast** (or a **sidearm cast**) to change the trajectory of the fly line to overcome the wind, throwing hard and tight, by lowering the angle of the fly rod just prior to releasing the line. A fly travels 200-plus miles per hour when casting with a graphite rod. Consequently, if you follow the basic straight-line casting tips and lower your trajectory a bit, you'll be able to cast into the wind.

Watch your back cast: Some anglers have a tendency not to pause long enough on the back cast to let the line stretch out, which creates what's called a "trailing loop" in the fly line that can cause it to crash during the forward casting stroke.

Good casting really boils down to knowing when to release the line. Practice fly casting, and remember famed American football coach Vince Lombardi's quote: "Practice does not make perfect. Only perfect practice makes perfect."

Fly Fishing with a Dry Fly

Fly fishing with a dry fly is often perceived as the ultimate fly fishing experience—there's nothing quite as satisfying as taking a fish on a well presented dry fly. For the most part, fishing with a dry fly falls in the domain of stream, not still-water fishing.

Gearing Up

If you intend to fly fish primarily on small streams, go with a 4-weight rod; go for a 5- or 6-weight rod for medium-size streams and a 7- or 8-weight rod for large streams. Choose matching floating fly line (weight forward). Tie some Dacron fly line backing on the end of your fly line and attach it to the reel, the amount being dependent on the capacity of your reel. Don't add more backing than you need so that the fly line strips easily from the spool.

A straight-line cast is most commonly used to deliver a dry fly on target.

Attach a tapered leader to the end of your fly line using the loop on the end of the fly line, or cut off the loop and use a nail knot to fasten the leader. Tapered leaders are ideal for presenting small, delicate flies; 9 feet is a good all around length. Next, tie the tippet to the end of the tapered leader using a double surgeon's knot. Normally, tippets are cut about 3 feet in length. Remember the "4 Rule" when selecting tippet size—divide the size of the fly hook by 4. Generally, 1X–3X will cover the bases for streams in Alberta and British Columbia.

Popular Patterns

There are three major taxonomic classes of aquatic insects that fish key in on when feeding: caddis flies, mayflies and stoneflies. Insects in these categories spend most of their life cycle in an aquatic stage as juveniles and only a short period of time in a terrestrial stage as adults, during which they mate and then lay eggs in the water. Caddis flies emerge from spring right up until autumn. Mayflies hatch primarily during summer and live for only a day as adults. Stoneflies are the first to emerge in spring, some species when there's still ice cover; other species emerge during summer.

Let 'em take it: A common phrase of dry fly anglers. When a fish rises towards a dry fly, it's often possible to see it swim towards the fly, and there's a temptation to set the hook before it actually swallows the fly. It's important to let the fish break water and close its mouth on the fly before raising the tip of your fly rod to set the hook.

Attractor patterns are always go-to dry flies.

Keen fly fishers often have dozens of dry flies to "match the hatch," which is jargon for using fly patterns that mimic whatever insects might be hatching. Hatches tend to be highly synchronized events: I recall witnessing a major hatch of stoneflies on the banks of the Peace River one evening that was of biblical proportions, featuring many thousands of emerging stoneflies. Often, there are few bugs in the air, especially during the day, because major insect hatches occur during the evening when winds tend to be calm.

If there's little sign of a hatch in progress, it's best to use attractor (search) patterns and large, gaudy flies that imitate adult stoneflies: Big Ugly, Turks Tarantula, Madame X, Chernobyl Ant, Stimulators and Water Walkers. Brown and Green Drakes and Parachute Adams, which imitate mayflies, are good other choices, as are Elk Hair Caddis patterns, Beatles or Hopper patterns, which imitate grasshoppers.

Casting Tips

Before you make your first cast, break down the water in front of you into imaginary grids, and systematically cover the water in each grid. Start by casting upstream near the bank and work your way out towards the middle of the stream.

You'll be surprised how many fish are up against the stream bank.

Then fish in front of you, repeating the process. You'll be surprised at how many trout will be at your feet, up against the stream bank. Obviously, you should focus on the most promising lairs as you search for trout: boulder gardens, pocket water, seams between runs and pools, foam lines, tail outs at the bottom of pools, deep runs and pools. Try to fly fish while heading in an upstream direction if possible.

Use a power (handshake) grip on the handle of the fly rod: thumb on top, fingers around the handle. Strip some fly line from your reel in preparation of a cast; hold it in your hand or let it fall at your feet. Next, make a roll cast to get the line in the water. A roll cast involves nothing more than flicking your wrist in a forward motion, which lifts the line off the ground and propels it forward. Once you've laid some line on the water with the roll cast, lift the tip of the rod and use a straight-line cast to gain some distance. Use short strokes for short casts and long strokes for long casts. Always pause on your back cast so you don't get a trailing loop. When you feel the line straighten out, punch the rod forward; stop when the tip of the rod is on the horizon and then let the line drop. It takes a lot of practice to get the hang of casting. It's all about rhythm.

It's critical to mend your line when fly fishing streams so you get a drag-free drift. The fly should float at the same speed as the current; otherwise it will be whipped forward. If you've played "crack the whip" when skating, that is what happens to a fly if the line isn't mended. When the fly lands on the water, lift the line and loop it upstream to create a drag-free drift.

Casting a dry fly is therapeutic, and even if you don't catch anything, you'll feel rewarded at the end of the day. There's just something about the rhythm that brings comfort to your soul.

Fly Fishing with Streamers

Although fly fishing with streamers isn't all that popular because the technique is hard to master, it's one of the most effective ways to catch many species of fish in both lakes and (in particular) medium to large streams.

Streamers are the ticket to catching really big fish, no matter where you're fishing. They're my go-to flies when I'm targeting large fish of the following species in Alberta: Arctic grayling, brook trout, brown trout, bull trout, cutthroat trout, goldeye, lake trout, northern pike and rainbow trout. Furthermore, if you plan to venture out and fly fish for Arctic char, salmon and steelhead, you simply must master the art of fly fishing with streamers. There's nothing fancy about fly fishing with streamers, but large streamers can be hard to cast, and it's essential to work the fly line while fishing with streamers.

Fly fishers should learn to fish with streamers if they're after big fish.

Gearing Up

I'd recommend an 8-weight, tip-flex, 9-foot fly fishing rod to fish streamers. This sort of rod is the most versatile variety on the market and will turn large flies over relatively easily. While you could use a lighter weight rod for streamer fishing, you'll be at a distinct handicap when targeting the larger species. It's not necessary to purchase a double-handed Spey rod to fly fish with streamers. A single-handed rod will get the job done. I would suggest purchasing a large-arbour fly fishing reel because the large spool makes it that much easier to reel in line quickly (an important feature when a large fish is on the end of the line) and to bring the fish under control quickly.

Streamers imitate bait fish and relatively large aquatic invertebrates. In flowing water they're usually (but not always) fished with a sink tip line, although shooting heads (i.e., Skagit lines) are the norm when fly fishing with streamers for salmon

and steelhead trout, whereas full sink lines are normally used in standing waters. Some of my fly angling friends believe the new Skandi lines are much easier to cast than Skagit lines.

Whether you're fly fishing in lakes (in shallow water) or streams, an intermediate sink tip line that matches your rod weight is usually fine in Alberta and British Columbia; it should be spooled with 100 yards of 20-pound test orange Dacron backing, which lets you see the backing in the water and locate a fish when it changes directions. You can overload your rod weight by spooling the next higher size of fly line to ease casting—for example, use a 9-weight line on an 8-weight rod.

Try for the money shot: The "money shot" is a place that appears most likely to hold some fish, it's usually fairly obvious—for example, at the top of a pool or along a seam of water separating a run from a pool.

You don't usually need tippet material; monofilament leader of an appropriate weight for your target species is adequate. Use 3 feet of leader. Make a perfection loop knot at one end of the leader to fasten it to the loop on the end of the fly line, or tie a nail knot if the line doesn't have a loop. The jury is out whether fluorocarbon is actually superior to monofilament leader when fly fishing with streamers.

You can use many different knots to tie a streamer to a leader. I use a double clinch knot, which will not fail. It's important to lubricate the knot with saliva or by dipping it in the water and then tighten it with a slow, steady pull to seat it properly, and then make sure it holds. Some fly fishermen use a Rapala knot, which they believe gives a streamer a more natural action in the water than other knots.

Popular Patterns

While there are many varieties of streamers, several will cover most of the bases for Alberta waters. The Woolly Bugger comes in many different styles and is black, olive or brown in colour. There have been numerous changes made to the Woolly Bugger fly pattern since it was first introduced; some are fashioned with cone heads, the shank may or may not be weighted, and some come with rubber legs. The Egg Sucking Leech is a popular streamer. A Marabou Leech pattern is another go-to streamer, and a consistent producer. The Mickey Finn and Muddler Minnow patterns have long been go-to streamers, especially in flowing water. The Muddler Minnow can be deadly on bull trout. The Hornberg Special is a Quebec streamer and one of my favourite flies for brook trout and rainbow trout. The Gartside Leech is one of the better streamers on the lower Bow River, along with the Bow River Bugger; both of these patterns come in various colours, any one of which might be effective on a given day.

You'll find it's often necessary to change colours when using streamers to get regular hook-ups. If you're after big pike and

A rainbow trout taken on a Bow River Bugger streamer.

Large grey or white deceiver streamers are excellent on lake trout.

lake trout, Rabbit Strip streamers are often the ticket to catch the largest fish, in black, brown and orange colours. Some colours seem to be more effective than others for pike; Chris Hanks, author of *Fly Fishing in the Northwest Territories of Canada*, said he'd pick either black or chartreuse if he could use only two colours. Large grey or white deceivers are dynamite on lake trout.

It can be awkward to cast large streamers and in particular those made of natural dressing. I suggest using streamers made of synthetic material instead of natural fibres unless you're going to troll them.

Casting Tips

When walk-and-wade fishing, pay attention to your casting stance, with your left leg forward if you're right-handed and your opposite leg forward for a power cast. Start by stripping some line off the reel. Use a roll cast to get the line in the water.

Then make a straight-line cast to gain some distance. After you've laid some line on the water, raise the rod and cast again, using the surface tension on the water to flex the rod as an aid in increasing the distance of your cast. Keep your false casts to a minimum when casting heavy streamers. Use a Belgian cast when pitching exceptionally large streamers: don't pause on your back cast, but rather, rotate your wrist to swing the fly line around in a fluid motion and then cast the streamer towards your target. It's a power cast for acquiring distance very quickly while casting large, heavy streamers or casting into the wind.

If you're fly fishing pools and runs in a stream, it's usually best to start at the top and cast across and down. Let the streamer swing in the current in a dead drift until it reaches the end of the line, twitching the streamer from time to time during the

Let streamers float in a dead drift and swing with the current.

drift. Take a few steps downstream and repeat the process until you reach the tail-out. Strip the fly during the retrieve once it has reached the end of its drift. Fish usually hook themselves when they strike a streamer; however, be sure to set the hook when you feel a strike.

In flowing water, mending is essential to many presentations; after you've made your cast, lift the fly line and throw it either upstream or downstream to mend or put a curve in the line. Mend as soon as your fly touches water. Mending is necessary to ensure a fly drifts naturally in the current in a dead drift, as though it's not attached to a fly line.

Cast a couple of times to see how the current affects the line. If the line races ahead of the fly, throw an upstream mend to slow the drift. Keep mending the fly, if necessary, to slow the drift. On the other hand, if the fly races ahead of the line, throw a downstream mend to slow the drift.

Try high sticking the streamer when fishing mid-water seams in a stream, and

cherry pick promising lies along stream banks, especially beside undercut banks or near root balls and logjams. High sticking simply involves holding the tip of a fly rod high in the air, at arm's length, and dancing a fly along or through promising holding water in a downstream direction so it doesn't snag on the stream bottom.

Always keep the tip of the rod pointed towards the fly in anticipation of a strike. Raise the rod tip a bit if you're getting into shallow water so you don't snag the bottom. Use a similar approach if you're casting from a boat when fishing on a lake.

If you're fly fishing with streamers from a drift boat or inflatable raft, you'll normally cast in a forward direction towards your target, which is often shallow water up against the stream bank. You should usually mend the line upstream when it hits the water to sink the streamer. You can then let the fly float in a dead drift until it finishes its swing before retrieving it in short strips (to create a porpoising action). Another option is to try to "swim" the fly alongside the drift boat or raft after casting the streamer to the shore and giving it a downstream mend depending on the speed of the current.

Because streamers are often big, heavy flies, they can be dangerous to cast. Be cautious when casting streamers; wear glasses to protect your eyes and a hat to protect your scalp.

Fly Fishing with a Nymph

"To nymph or not to nymph" is a hotly debated topic among fly fishing aficionados because it's deemed the dark side of the sport by elitist fly fishers. I'm not sure how the image of nymphing got tarnished, but tarnished it is, for no good reason.

Some fly fishers tend to get frustrated when fishing with streamers or dry flies. If they don't get a lot of action, they switch to using nymphs. Fishing with nymphs is so similar to bait fishing with a pole that

I guess detractors think that it's not very challenging. The diehard streamer and dry fly anglers seem to prefer to go down with the ship regardless of the merits of nymphs.

Granted, fly fishing with a nymph may require less skill than fly fishing with a dry fly or streamers, but that's no reason to relegate it to the back page. It's certainly a great way to catch all manner of trout, Arctic char, Arctic grayling and mountain whitefish.

Fly fishing with a nymph on flowing waters is comparable to fishing with a cork or plastic float back in the day when it was legal to use bait in flowing waters. For still water, it's a rare day when a fly fisher would consider using a dry fly, although streamers certainly can be very productive. If you want to consistently catch fish, however, nymphs are a good bet because they imitate many aquatic invertebrates that are common prey of trout, in particular, and are easy to use with a bit of practice.

Nymphs can be productive when dry flies are not.

Use a 6-weight fly rod with a mid-arbour reel loaded with a floating line.

Gearing Up

For still water, I'd opt for a 5- or 6-weight, mid-flex fly rod, which is suitable for a wide range of conditions and casting styles, rigged with a mid-arbour reel spooled with a floating line, an appropriate-sized tapered leader for the size of your quarry with a relatively long tippet (i.e., 8–10 feet), and a strike indicator. There are many strike indicators on the market and all have their pros and cons, but brightly coloured, miniature plastic bobber indicators are probably best for still waters because of their visibility.

For flowing water, again I'd opt for a 5- or 6-weight mid-flex fly rod rigged with a mid-arbour reel spooled with a floating line and an appropriate-sized tapered leader for the size of your quarry, but with a short tippet (i.e., 2–3 feet), with or without a strike indicator. The snobbish side of fly fishers enters the equation at this point once again. Some fly fishers look down on those who would use a strike indicator as

though they're Neanderthals or something worse. Talk about discrimination. If you feel comfortable using a strike indicator, by all means use one; if not, you'll be okay fishing without one, although they do take the guess work out of strikes.

Brightly coloured, pinch-on foam strike indicators are popular because they're small and easy to use, plus they're practically weightless, so they don't impede casting. Yarn indicators are very popular simple strike indicators and are made of synthetic or wool yarns. These are treated with a waterproofing agent that will allow the indicator to ride on the water's surface for many hours. Most yarn indicators are attached to the line by looping the leader material around the float using a slip knot. Adjust the position of strike indicator on your leader for the depth of water you're fishing; make an allowance for parallax because the water will always be deeper than perceived by the human eye.

Popular Patterns

You don't need a host of different nymphs when fly fishing still waters. Chironomids are always a good choice, although Double Shrimps and various bead head nymphs (i.e., bead head Prince, Pheasant Tail and Hare's Ear nymphs) are all close behind. There are several searching nymphs, for example dark halfbacks, that are also producers. These would normally be fished without a strike indicator, but rather by casting into promising lairs and retrieving them with short strips.

There are lots of nymphs that will catch trout, char, grayling and mountain whitefish in streams. Some of the most popular nymphs for flowing water are the Copper John, bead head Prince, Pheasant Tail and Hare's Ear nymphs, and the San Juan

worm. Additionally, there are literally dozens of mayfly and stonefly nymph patterns that will catch fish, with the Golden Stone being an old standby.

Casting Tips

The salient question is always, where do you actually go fishing on still waters? The littoral area along the shoreline is generally your best bet, especially in bays, and in channels between islands, along points that jut into the lake and near underwater structures such as boulders and sunken logs where trout and char can find some sanctuary. When in doubt, look for insect hatches to narrow your search because trout will never be far away. Pupal cases (i.e., insect shucks) on the water's surface are a good sign of recent hatches, as are swallows flying low over the water. Insect

A fly box with a selection of bead head nymphs in the centre.

hatches can occur at any time during the day but are most common in the evening when winds are calm.

Plastic bobber indicators can create some casting issues for inexperienced fly fishers because they're unstable aerodynamically—they're a bit like having an anchor on your fly line. To compensate for the interference caused by the plastic bobber, I suggest that you initially lay some line out with a roll cast when fishing from a boat or float tube, then use the surface tension to load the fly rod before you make a straight line cast to your target.

It's difficult to fly fish pocket water when using nymphs where dry flies are much better suited because they float high in the water. However, you'll catch lots of fish using nymphs in runs and pools, especially in the morning and early afternoon when rises are infrequent.

Cast across and down into promising holding water, let the fly float in a dead drift, and keep your eye on the strike indicator (if you're using one). If the strike indicator suddenly sinks or moves laterally, raise the tip of your fly rod and set the hook. If you're not using a strike indicator, simply handle your fly line at all times so you can sense a strike.

Fly Fishing with a Wet Fly

Wet flies are an old-fashioned type of fly pattern. For some reason, fly fishing with a wet fly isn't as popular nowadays as it used to be in Alberta, but it's still very much in vogue in British Columbia and remains the *modus operandi* for Atlantic salmon aficionados in eastern Canada. When I was a kid I used to fish with wet flies all the time, as did most of my buddies. Wet flies imitate aquatic insects, and the soft hackle on their thorax buoys them and makes them look like insects as they float in a current.

Cast across and down when fly fishing nymphs in streams.

Wet flies will take rainbows and cutthroat trout.

Gearing Up

The rod weight of choice will of course vary depending on the size of your quarry; however, for most practical purposes, a 6-weight rod is ideal for trout and mountain whitefish in western Canada, while an 8-weight rod is okay for most Atlantic salmon fishing in eastern Canada. A mid-arbour reel is a good match for a 6-weight rod; use a large-arbour reel for an 8-weight rod. Normally, a floating line with a 9-foot tapered leader is used when fishing with wet flies. No strike indicator is necessary; a tap on the line signals a bite.

Streams tend to be gin clear in Alberta and British Columbia whereas they're usually stained the colour of tea out east—but not always, depending on the drainage. Consequently, the jury is out regarding fluorocarbon leaders as compared with regular monofilament leaders, the latter being adequate in most cases.

Popular Patterns

Some of the more popular wet fly patterns in Alberta and British Columbia are the Adams, Black Gnat, Brown Hackle, Doc Spratley, Golden Stone, Grizzly King, Light Cahill and Royal Coachman. The Brown Hackle and Royal Coachman, when tipped with a maggot where permitted by law, are deadly on mountain whitefish and will also do the job on trout in Alberta's east slope streams.

In eastern Canada, there are several go-to wet flies used for Atlantic salmon fly fishing: Blue Charm, Green Machine and several variations of the Thunder and Lightning pattern. The Hornberg is an old Quebec wet fly pattern that's especially popular in eastern Canada for brook trout. I've had good success with this pattern on rainbow and cutthroat trout in Alberta. There are several variations of Hornberg fly patterns; the earliest Hornberg pattern was a wet fly, but more recently this has been tied as a streamer pattern. There are literally dozens of other wet fly patterns produced regionally, too numerous to mention.

Some popular Atlantic salmon wet fly patterns.

Cast wet flies across and down.

Casting Tips

Wet flies are typically fished in flowing, not still water. Freestone streams in the west tend to have rather steep gradients compared with those in eastern Canada, so the fly fishing technique varies for wet flies from west to east. A weighted wet fly might be necessary on relatively deep, fast moving western streams, whereas a non-weighted wet fly should be okay in the east. If you were to fish with a weighted fly in the east, you'd likely be snagged on the bottom most of the day.

The secret to not getting snagged is to high stick your fly through holding water, with the rod held at shoulder level in an elevated position in the west, while simply tilting your arm and the rod tip at a 45-degree angle would normally be adequate in the east. A rule of thumb is to point the tip of a fly rod towards a fly as it drifts downstream to get good hook sets.

The standard cast when fly fishing with a wet fly is typically in an "across and down" direction. On large streams, make your cast at a 45-degree angle across the stream, then let the wet fly swing in the current while keeping the tip of the rod at an angle of a least 45 degrees. Stay engaged as the fly drifts in the current, then strip line on the retrieve once it completes its swing. You could cast straight across on smaller streams.

Mending is necessary whenever fly fishing in running water to try to achieve a dead drift, the most natural float possible. Typically, an upstream mend would be necessary when the fly lands in the water by raising the rod out of the water as the fly lands and lifting the line upstream (in a curve). The upstream curve in the line would prevent the fly from racing downstream faster than the speed of the current. If there is slack water in front of you, however, you'll have to make a downstream mend to achieve a dead drift; otherwise the current will quickly sweep the line downstream and the fly will rocket forward faster than the current as if whiplashed while drifting downstream.

Staying engaged as the wet fly drifts in the current simply means keeping a finger on the line to detect any strikes, which can be subtle. If you feel a tug, set the hook by raising the tip of your rod. As with any kind of fly fishing, you'll be making a lot of casts, so keep your fly line clean and treated before each outing.

Landing Mr. Big

If you're lucky, every once in a while you're going to hook a really big fish. Over the past several years I've been fortunate to land some personal bests on a fly rod: Arctic char, coho, steelhead, northern pike, brook trout, Arctic grayling, lake trout,

cutthroat trout, brown trout, rainbows and bull trout. What should you do to increase the chances of landing a really big fish on a fly rod, and how does this vary from species to species, from the initial hook set to bringing it to reel, playing the fish and finally landing it, whether in a landing net or fish cradle?

Many large fish are lost either within moments of being hooked or at the tail end of the battle just as they're being landed. How should you handle a fly rod in those critical moments just after the hook set, and what shouldn't you do in trying to bring the fish to reel? What about actually landing a large fish; how do you bring it to a net or fish cradle in a stream or lake without dislodging the hook, or having the fish throw the hook? With most of Canada under barbless hook regulations, you must understand how to play a fish caught with a barbless hook because quite often that little barb is all that holds the fly in the jaw or mouth of a fish.

The author with a coho salmon on the Extew River, BC, in 2011.

Lake trout have tough jaws, so it's necessary to ensure a good hook set.

For starters, regardless of whether you're fishing a lake or stream, and no matter what kind of species you're fishing for, the most important thing is having a razor sharp hook, especially for big, tough-jawed fish like Arctic char, bull trout, lake trout and northern pike. Always check the tip of your fishing hook to make sure it has a sharp edge, and use a hand-held sharpening stone to ensure it keeps an edge if it starts to wear off. This step is particularly important after having a bottom snag or two on rocky substrates, which can easily dull the tip of the hook.

Next, make sure that the hook is properly tied to your tippet or leader so the knot won't slip—in the case of fly fishing lines, use the Albright knot to secure the fly line to the backing and use a nail knot or the loop on the end of the fly line to tie the leader. I recommend a minimum of 100 yards of backing when chasing large fish such as Arctic char, bull trout and lake trout and even for large pike, although they usually don't run far. There are many knots that can be used to tie a fly or lure to the end of your line. I favour a clinch knot, which is easy to tie and has never failed me, although other knots such as the double clinch and Palomar knot are regarded as even stronger. When using braided line, it's also a good idea to melt the tip of the tag line with a butane lighter or match to ensure there's no possible slippage, regardless of whether you use a clinch, double clinch or Palomar knot because knots in braided lines have a tendency to wiggle loose.

When a really big fish strikes a fly—an Arctic char, bull trout, lake trout or pike, in particular—you must set the hook with attitude; in fact, I yard on it to make sure the fly sticks. This won't be a problem if you're using a short 15- to 20-pound monofilament leader because you'll most likely be using a large streamer fly, which can take a good, solid hook set and won't bend.

On relatively small trout and Arctic grayling, it's advisable to first bring the fish under control by handling it with the fly line until it settles down before trying to bring it reel. But after hooking large char, pike and trout, it's best to capitalize on the breaking power of your reel and minimize handling them by line. It's absolutely essential to try to bring a big fish to reel as soon as possible; otherwise you'll cut your hand on the fly line, or worse, break the tip of your rod. A large-arbour reel is a definite asset when trying to control large pike in particular, which are really ferocious,

dangerous fish that strike aggressively and with a vengeance, because you can bring in that much more fly line quickly. Use the drag on the reel, the flex in the fly rod and the stretch in the fly line to tire really large fish before trying to land them.

It's only natural to get excited when you have a brute on the end of the line, but don't get over-excited or you'll lose the fish before the battle really starts. Never horse a large fish because it may throw the hook, or the line or the rod tip may break, or your reel may come apart. Once you've brought the fish to reel, begin to play it out before trying to land it. The proper technique at this stage is pretty straightforward: when the fish runs, give it some line; when it stops its run, pump your rod and slowly reel it in. Repeat the process until the fish tires. Never set the drag too tight or the line will snap. Keep your rod tip high to ensure there's some tension on the end of the line, which makes it hard for a fish to throw

It's essential to bring large pike to reel as quickly as possible, or they'll throw a hook.

a hook. Be careful if the fish runs towards you because your line will go slack and you'll be in danger of losing the fish. Be prepared to reel in line fast, or hand strip your fly line and keep your rod tip at an even greater height if this happens.

> *Keep a tight line: It's necessary to maintain constant pressure on a fishing line once a fish is hooked, or it will toss it and escape; however, when fly fishing, there's a delicate balance at play because if too much pressure is applied, the tippet will break.*

In a stream, a hooked Arctic grayling, char or trout will avoid an angler, shying away from a drift boat or rubber raft. They often seek the depths of a pool or make for a current or underwater structure. Under

these circumstances, give them some line until they settle into a comfort zone before trying to reel them in. The flex of the fly rod and drag of the reel will eventually tire them, and they can be landed when they're sufficiently tired.

When attempting to net your trophy or guide it into a fish cradle, do not apply any more pressure on the end of your line than necessary—excess pressure is potentially dangerous and can cause the hook to become dislodged, flip up and hit your partner in the face. It's also a good way to break the tip of your rod. While you're applying pressure in an upwards direction to bring the fish towards the net (or cradle), your partner should slide the net under the fish and scoop it up from underneath. If you're fishing from a drift boat or rubber raft in a stream, it's usually best to beach the craft and try to land the fish from shore, where there's less danger of having your line caught up on the oars or other paraphernalia. On lakes, do not let

Large Arctic char have an incredible burst speed, so let them run and take to the chase if necessary.

Use large streamers to catch the largest fish, and fish smart to save your casting arm.

a large fish get underneath a boat, or it will probably break your rod. Likewise, do whatever is necessary to keep it away from the motor so the line doesn't get tangled in the propeller.

A word about flies—while there's no universal rule related to the absolute size of flies and fish caught, generally speaking, the larger the fly, the larger the fish, with some exceptions. When I'm fly fishing for large char, pike and trout, I almost always use large streamers, often weighted with cone heads or dumbbell eyes. Having said that, some of the largest fish I've ever caught fly fishing have been on relatively small streamers. In these cases, the streamer patterns have imitated forage fish or leaches.

In flowing water, whether you're fly fishing for Arctic grayling, char or trout, streamers will almost always catch the largest fish—

well-known patterns such as Woolly Buggers, Mickey Finn, Matuka, Clouser Minnows and the Bow River Bugger are all go-to flies. While gaudy colours sometimes work well for these patterns, my first choice would be subtle, natural colours such as black, brown and olive, especially if the bite is slow. You may not catch a lot of fish under these circumstances, but the ones you do catch will often be quite large—it's all a matter of patience and perseverance when streamer fishing.

Because you'll usually be using large streamers when fly fishing for large fish, you have to fish smart to save your casting arm; otherwise you'll get played out before the day is done. On guided trips, it's not unusual to fish for more than seven hours daily. If I'm casting streamers, I use the water to load the fly rod to increase my casting range and lengthen my casts until

I'm on target. Make a short cast, let the fly line lie in the water, lift the rod to retrieve it and cast again until you've achieved the desired range. If you don't use the surface tension on the water to load your fly rod, you'll almost certainly tire yourself out and maybe end up with a bad case of tendonitis if you're pitching large streamers. You can also troll, very effectively, when fly fishing with large streamers—just remember to power strip your line from time to time to entice strikes. Or you can use the wind drift if it's not too choppy when fly fishing from a boat.

With the above tips in mind, you're ready to land Mr. Big. Granted, it will take some practice.

Fishing Highs and Lows: Water Temperature Matters

Like humans, fish have a temperature comfort zone; knowledge of this zone will help improve your catches. If it's too hot, fishing drops off, and same for when it's too cold. So what should you do before planning your day's strategy?

It helps to develop an understanding of the temperature dynamics in foothills and mountain streams where most trout and Arctic grayling reside (i.e., the diurnal cycle), as well as an understanding of the annual temperature regime in lakes (i.e., summer stratification; the autumnal turnover; winter homeostasis; spring warm-up) and how these temperature cycles have a bearing on fish distribution and feeding activity.

From May to October, the water temperature in freestone rivers in the foothills and mountains of Alberta and British Columbia (and even large rivers on the prairies) typically goes through a predictable daily cycle. Temperatures will cool overnight and then warm up during the day. On a freestone river, temperatures might cool to 5–10° C (or less) overnight during July and August and then warm up to 15–20° C (or more) during the afternoon and evening—a range of about 10 degrees in temperature during the day is normal. In May and June, temperatures might cool to near 0° C overnight and peak at 5–10° C later on in the day. Water temperatures will be in the same

Stream temperatures go through a predictable daily cycle in the Rocky Mountains.

range during September and October as they were in May and June. Under winter ice, water temperatures will be about 1° C on streams and rivers in western Canada.

Lakes go through less-pronounced daily temperature fluctuations than streams, and their temperatures change slowly through the seasons. The normal annual temperature cycle of a lake follows the same pattern throughout Canada. In winter, ice will be near 0° C—ice floats because it has a density less than that of water. Below the ice, the temperature to the bottom is much the same, in the range of 1–2° C. Once the ice melts in spring and the surface temperature warms to 4° C, mixing will begin as the dense 4° C water sinks to the bottom (water is at its maximum density at 4° C), and for a short while the lake will uniformly become 4° C. As spring turns to summer, winds cause the transfer of heat from the surface water, as it warms, to deeper water, and most lakes become thermally stratified during summer. That is, the surface temperatures are warmer than the bottom temperatures. During summer, water temperatures are generally in the range of

15–20° C at the surface and 4° C in the bottom layer beneath the "thermocline," which is a transition zone between warm upper layers and cold bottom layers. This is a very stable temperature regime that will persist until autumn, when surface temperatures cool to 4° C and mixing takes place again.

When fly fishing, always start the day by taking the water temperature, and make a habit of doing this. I usually take the water temperature as a matter of course before I start fishing to give me a clue as to what kind of tackle might be best, and to see if I'm in the strike zone, so to speak. This simple task will take some of the mystery out of catching fish, whether you're on a lake or a stream. When the water is really cold (e.g., 4–5° C) don't expect red-hot action, although there will be some feeding activity. Same for when the water is quite warm (20° C or higher). Pocket thermometers can be obtained from many tackle shops and/or supply catalogues.

Take the following scenario by way of example. A few years ago, I was fishing for lake trout with my partner, Chuck Anderson, on Wellesley Lake, Yukon, out of

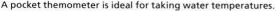

A pocket themometer is ideal for taking water temperatures.

Kluane Wilderness Lodge. The surface water temperature was 12° C, so I mentioned to Chuck that we'd probably have to go deep if we expected any action. Why? Simply because lake trout tend to head for cooler, deep water when surface water temperatures reach 13° C. I returned my thermometer to a safe place in my vest after taking a surface temperature reading early in the afternoon, knowing full well that the temperature would rise a bit as the day wore on and I wouldn't need it again. The absolute preferred temperature of lake trout is 10° C, so at least we were in the ball park. It wasn't long before I had my first strike, at a depth of 24 feet, after letting out about 60 feet of fast sinking fly line and

20-odd feet of backing. The strike zone on this overcast day in mid-June was from 20 to 30 feet deep, and that's where we targeted the lake trout.

Have you heard that cutthroats are for sleepy heads? Well, they are; it's not necessary to get up at the crack of dawn to get some hook-ups on cutties. To the contrary, some of the best action could well be in the afternoon or during the evening. Why? Water temperatures are cool in the morning in mountain streams, and cutthroats' preferred temperatures don't roll around until later on in the day once the sun warms the water. You will catch some fish in the morning, but you'll catch more in the afternoon.

Cutthroat trout don't start feeding actively until the water temperature rises in the afternoon.

Soucie's Field Guide of Fishing Facts lists the preferred temperatures of some fish:

Fish	°C	°F
Lake trout	4–13	40–55
Brook trout	7–16	45–61
Arctic char	11–16	53–61
Arctic grayling	8–11	47–52
Steelhead	9–11	48–52
Mountain whitefish	9–11	48–52
Lake whitefish	11	52
Kokanee	10–15	50–59
Atlantic salmon	10–17	50–62
Cutthroat trout	10–18	50–65
Rainbow trout	10–21	50–70
Brown trout	13–18	55–65
Northern pike	13–18	55–65
Walleye	15–20	59–68
Yellow perch	19–25	66–77
Goldeye	21+	70+

Note: The guide does not list a low temperature for lake whitefish, but it would likely be in the same range as for mountain whitefish.

Refer to the preferred temperature chart. You'll notice that I've listed the char species (Arctic char, brook trout and lake trout) at the top of the list, and "warm water" species (perch, pike, walleye and goldeye) near the bottom, with whitefish and the true trout in the middle of the chart. Members of the char family like cold water and are just waiting for the next Ice Age to break out; they can be taken quite readily in the morning, whereas you're better off trying to catch cutthroat and rain-bow trout later on in the day—depending on where you're fishing and whether it's a lake or a stream.

All bets are off if there have been any significant local weather disturbances just before or during your fishing trip that might cool the water. For example, periods of rain, even if only a thundershower or two, will have an impact. This doesn't mean you should necessarily stop fishing for species such as cutthroat trout, but if you're fly fishing, action might be slow on dry flies, and switching to nymphs (or streamers) could pay off until the day wears on. Likewise, if you're fishing either early in the season or late in the season, dry flies might be a poor choice, while a nymph or a streamer might be better producers; if they fail, switch to a wet fly.

Fish will feed regardless of the water temperature and are actually the only vertebrate that doesn't stop growing until they die. If temperatures are low, however, they will not feed very often because their metabolism is slow, and they will also be rather sluggish. If you've ever ice fished, you'll have no doubt noted that the fish don't attack a lure with a lot of speed, and they don't fight as much on the end of a line, compared with the open water period—same for most species of fish caught in early spring. On another note,

if the temperatures are high, they will likewise be sluggish, and for some species such as rainbow trout, temperatures above 25° C can be lethal.

We've dealt with the prime fishing season during summer; now what about spring and autumn? After ice breakup, temperatures will be universally cool in both flowing and standing water, often near 5–6° C, so don't expect red-hot action; it just won't happen until temperatures rise later on in spring. You'll catch fish, but not a lot of them.

In the case of autumn, however, temperatures may well be ideal throughout the day for many sought-after species. For example, when fishing for Atlantic salmon out of Pond's Resort on the Miramichi River in New Brunswick, daytime water temperatures were

Lake trout have a preferred water temperature of 10° C.

Fall produces ideal temperatures for catching Atlantic salmon in New Brunswick.

13–14° C from 9:00 AM to 7:00 PM, right in the middle of their preferred temperature range, which translated into potential hook-ups all day long. Our reward was some fine salmon during that trip.

I've enjoyed the same kind of success on cutthroat trout streams in Alberta and British Columbia in September under similar circumstances because the water temperature was ideal all day long. On the other hand, during an outing with Reel Fishing Adventures on the Athabasca River in early October one year, the water temperature remained at 10° C throughout the day. The fallout was slow fishing for walleye, but not without at least some hook-ups.

And now you know the story: why angling can often be so good during autumn. Water temperatures aren't strictly definitive when it comes to forecasting fishing success, but they are very important. If you make a habit of measuring the water temperature, you will have a good idea of the type of strategy and tactics you should employ.

Chapter 3

Fly Fishing in Moving Water

Listen to the sound of the river and you will get a trout.
—Irish proverb

How to Read and Fly Fish a Trout Stream

Fly fishing neophytes often wonder how to read a trout stream; many ponder where, when and how to cast a fly. Wayne Gretzky once said, "I skate to where the puck is going to be, not where it has been." Reading water in a trout stream is a bit like playing hockey because conditions can, and do, change while trout move about their home range. Where are the fish holed up under

such dynamic conditions? Experienced fly fishers know that fish seek stability, and that trout try to find a comfort zone under either stable or unstable conditions.

In late autumn and winter, trout and mountain whitefish will move into select overwintering pools that are deep, with slow-moving currents. Here they spend some six to eight months of the year until ice breakup. Native species of rainbow trout and cutthroat trout spawn during late

One of the best places to catch trout during the late summer is along a stream bank, where they wait for fallen grasshoppers.

May and early June. For the most part, this spawning activity takes place at the tail end of pools where clean gravel is present. In my experience, trout don't tend to feed much during the spawning period, which is often just before or just after the peak runoff. For the rest of the year, trout are present in all areas of a stream, particularly pocket water during the prime fishing period throughout the summer months, and on into September and early October.

Flows are slowest near the stream bottom, adjacent to stream banks, below boulders and at the tail-out of pools, all of which translate into good holding water; flows are fastest in the mid-water column, which is not ideal holding water. Holding water conditions vary depending on the annual discharge cycle, changes in stream temperature and amounts of dissolved oxygen in the stream. For example, cold water holds more dissolved oxygen than warm water, and trout will seek out oxygenated water. Likewise, the daily cycle of invertebrate drift in streams influences where trout are found throughout the day, as well as the seasonal abundance of terrestrial insects, both of which influence fish distribution.

For a typical stream, I'd use a 4- to 6-weight rod rigged with a 2- to 3-foot tippet on a 9-foot tapered leader. I'd use a floating line on a small stream, whereas a sink tip would be my choice on a larger stream.

Before noon, I'd use a searching nymph with or without a strike indicator depending on the size of the stream. Popular searching nymphs are the Prince Nymph and Pheasant Tails; bead head nymphs are my first choice because they reflect light, which attracts fish. The reason I'd fish with a nymph in the morning is quite simple. Trout tend to feed most actively on invertebrate drift during the morning because

that's when insects are most abundant in the water column. Invertebrate drift is a phenomenon characterized by a peak in aquatic insect activity during the night, when the majority of aquatic insects will be dislodged from their normal hiding areas in the gravel, under rocks and boulders as they scurry about the surface of these substrates while feeding. It tapers off during the daylight hours. Most insect hatches take place late in the day when winds are calm; consequently, there's usually little surface activity until at least early afternoon, if not later on during the evening.

If I was fishing in the afternoon, I'd select a dry fly: an attractor (or search) pattern such as an Adams, Madame X, Turk's Tarantula, Stimulator or Chernobyl Ant. These patterns are highly visible and float high in the water. They imitate terrestrial insects and adult aquatic insects common to BC and Alberta's trout streams during summer months. They're used to attract actively feeding fish.

You'll only need an ant: Fernie, BC, area fishing guide John Avery has popularized this saying, joking that the only fly pattern you really need is a Chernobyl ant when fly fishing for cutthroat trout in the Kootenay Rockies.

In the evening, I'd try to match the hatch of aquatic insects, which tends to occur more or less daily on trout streams in summer and autumn. Caddis fly imitations, mayflies and stoneflies are most common during this time in Alberta and British Columbia.

Learning to read a stream.

Reading the Stream

Let's first examine a photo of a typical trout stream with summer flows. Where do you think the best spots to catch a trout are in the above photo, and where should you cast? One of the first things a fly fisher must do before making a cast is break the stream down into imaginary grids. Subsequently, it's necessary to make successive casts into various grids without lining trout in an adjacent grid because this might inadvertently frighten them into hiding spots or turn them off feeding.

1. I'd make my first cast right along the stream bank below the fallen log on the left side of the photo. You'd be surprised at how many trout will lurk right beside a stream bank. Next I'd cast below and along the log. Logs offer overhead cover for trout, which are ever wary of avian predators such as herons, mergansers and

kingfishers. Pinpoint casts are essential. It takes a lot of practice and skill to make such casts and not get snagged on the branches on the top of this particular log.

2. My next casts would be below the notch between the log and this boulder, then just below the boulder in the centre of the photo. The notch would funnel insects floating on the surface and subsurface invertebrates in the drift into the pool downstream of the boulder. I'd bounce a fly off the boulder and let it drop into the pool.

3. I'd subsequently cast along the seam between the pool below the large boulder and the riffle to the right of the boulder, right along the foam line. This is probably the money shot where you're most likely to catch a trout. They would find sanctuary in the deep water of the pool (in relatively still water) but could scoot into the seam

to feed on aquatic insects that drift by, either on the surface or underwater.

4. Most trout would be in the riffle to the right of the pool (below the large rock) on a warm summer day. The riffle will be more oxygenated than anywhere else due to its turbulence and would consequently hold the most fish. I'd make my final casts along the left, downstream bank (on the right side of the riffle) and try to entice a rise from trout that might be holding along the edge of the stream bank.

Let's move on to other hidey-holes that are go-to spots for fly fishing trout streams, starting with fallen logs adjacent to stream banks, as in the case of the photo below.

1. I'd bet money that a few trout will be lurking underneath the log in this photo.

2. The trick will be to catch them because of the relatively slack water along the stream bank and the fast, turbulent current below the boulders in the lower right-hand part of the photo, which will make drag-free drifts a challenge.

3. I'd suggest high sticking an attractor pattern along the edge of the log to get a rise.

4. Don't overlook the small pocket water between the turbulent white water downstream of the boulders, which might also hold some fish.

Reading a logjam.

Reading a fallen log.

In the third photo, above, the water underneath the logjam and the adjacent pool are the most likely spots to hold fish, particularly when flows subside in summer and autumn.

1. The pool would be best fished with a highly visible attractor pattern in a dead drift.

2. If this doesn't get a rise, skate the fly in short strips over the surface of the pool.

Reading a plunge pool.

In the photo above, the plunge pool below a rock outcrop represents great holding water for trout.

1. Fish the pool from left to right with short straight-line casts to get drag-free drifts, from a downstream position.

2. Cast into the water along the seams between the quiet waters of the pool and the turbulent water characterized by bubbles for best results, especially under the foam line on the left side of the photo.

These are some basic tips on how to read a trout stream and fly fish it effectively. It's up to you to put these tips into practice if you want to get consistent hook-ups when stream fishing.

Fish at Your Feet

Several years ago, on a pleasant September day, I caught three 14- to 17-inch cutthroat trout in the Elk River, British Columbia, on the very first bend just downstream of one of the more popular drift boat launch sites—not five minutes after the start of a float trip—in mid-morning, in shirt-sleeve weather. All of these fish were caught virtually "at my feet" after clients in two other drift boats had already fly fished this bend in the river. Over the next two days, from early in the morning until the sun set, I was to catch many other trout under similar circumstances both from a drift boat and while walk-and-wade fly fishing on the Elk River. This wasn't just a matter of dumb luck. My son, Myles, had similar good fortune.

Believe it or not, when fly fishing on streams, you'll catch all manner of trout at your feet. And it's not just on large rivers such as the Elk or Alberta's Bow River. I've enjoyed similar success catching trout on many small streams and rivers in the foot-hills and mountains of Alberta and British Columbia—not to mention the odd moun-tain whitefish.

You'd be surprised at how many fine trout hug the stream bank.

It's common for trout to be in shallow water beside a fallen log.

Trout often spend a good part of the day in shallow water near stream banks—sometimes just inches away, in fact. The velocity of the current adjacent to stream banks is generally lower than in the midsection of a stream, as well as it being lower near the stream bottom, particularly where some structure is present that creates drag, such as rocks and boulders. These areas of microhabitat, as well as sections with a lot of pocket water, are preferred by trout in mountain streams.

Trout are often found in these situations particularly before noon and then again in the evening once the sun sets. While trout are ever wary of avian predators (e.g., kingfishers, herons, mergansers) and members of the weasel family (mink, otters) during the day, they will move to backwaters and shallow water on feeding forays at any

time. Also, in late summer, trout often hug stream banks in search of grasshoppers and beetles that fall or fly into streams—pay attention to these areas. As the sun sets, trout let their guard down and move to shallow pools and riffles to capitalize on the evening hatch of tiny mayflies, particularly blue-winged olives. It's not uncommon to find pods of cutthroat trout slurping emerging insects under these conditions, again, literally at your feet. If you pay attention, you'll be able to spot feeding trout and plan your strategy. Or you can simply play the odds, as you must when fishing from a fast-moving drift boat, and target likely holding areas up tight against a stream bank, for example.

So, how do you go about catching these fish? If you are on a walk-and-wade fishing trip, make a habit of looking for trout. Start by actively looking for trout in the shallows. It makes a big difference if you wear polarized sun glasses—they reduce the glare off the water, and you can see into the water and spot cruising trout. If you pay attention you will often see trout that make forays into shallow water at any time during the day. I once caught an 18-inch cutthroat trout on the St. Mary River in British Columbia by first spotting the fish while it was on a foray into the shallows a few feet away from where I was standing. I waited until it made its way back into the current and then plopped a fly in front of it. I caught it on my first cast.

Always watch for rises, as well as for the backs of trout breaching the water, particularly in seams between fast water and pools. Be sure to search for trout along foam lines, in pocket water associated with boulders (both submerged and exposed), among woody debris along stream banks and at the tail end of pools. These trout generally don't surface like a Trident missile. Rather, they usually gently breach the surface of the water with barely a ripple and then descend to their lair. Often you'll only spot their back. Sight cast for these fish, using short casts. Don't pound the water. You have to finesse fish at your feet, or you'll put them down. You may get only one chance to catch them, so make it count.

Foam is home: One of Bellevue, Alberta, Crowsnest Fly Shop owner and guide Vic Bergman's favourite sayings, it means to cast on top of foam lines to lure the skulking trout that find sanctuary underneath foam.

Sight cast to fish in pools (above) and in seams in fast water (right).

A basic straight-line cast, which is the most commonly used method of presenting a fly, works well when sight casting for fish in pools or in seams in fast water. The straight-line cast is performed by making a high back cast. Then, throw a good forward loop and follow the line almost to the water with the tip of your rod. Use just enough power to lay the line out straight. If you use too much thrust, the line will bounce back at you, creating slack line that may cause you to miss a strike. Strip any excess line as the fly drifts towards you, and get ready for a rise. I find that short straight-line casts work best when fishing for trout at your feet, if you are casting in an upstream direction.

A slack-line cast is a great downstream fishing technique when casting to a fish that is holding close to the bank. Start the slack-line cast with a high back cast and a tight forward loop. As the line turns over in front of you, wiggle the rod tip from side to side. This will cause the line to fall in a series of slack, s-shaped curves. Drop your rod tip as the line settles in the water and keep it pointed towards the fly. The current will play out the line as it heads towards the trout. Pay attention as the line plays out so you are ready to set the hook if a fish strikes.

While there are many ways to fish pocket water, which is associated with rocks and boulders, probably the easiest is to use a "dappling the fly" approach. This works best in turbulent water where trout can't see very well, and you can approach to a rod's length without scaring them. Simply poke the tip of your rod over a rock and dap the fly on the water's surface, allowing it to drift freely and without drag. Strikes are often instantaneous and sometimes explosive—hang onto your rod! You could also use a stack cast in this situation. Over-power the cast directly at the pocket water, and let out more line than you would on a straight-line cast. The extra line piles behind the fly, creating a short drag-free float. Cast to the right or left side of the main current, draping the fly over rocks and boulders, where necessary. For more on pocket water, see page 65.

A reach cast works well when a quick upstream or downstream mend of the line is required, especially for fast-moving water near stream banks or logjams. It's also effective when working a wet fly on a downstream swing when "nymphing" for trout, by "swimming" the fly. The reach cast is performed by moving the rod tip to the right or left as the fly line hits the water, when cast at right angles towards the target. The fly lands where you have cast it, but the back of the line settles onto the water either to your right or left (upstream or downstream). When making a reach cast, be sure to let a bit of slack out as you swing the rod to the left or right. Follow through by mending your line as often as necessary to minimize any drag and get a natural drift.

It's absolutely critical to mend once, twice or even three times when fly fishing for trout at your feet. And don't be afraid to dance the fly. Fish all the water in front of you starting at the bank. Don't wade until you've finished fishing the area adjacent to the stream bank. You may have to go down to a 5X tippet in clear mountain streams and use tiny flies to get a strike, but that's all part of the fun. Fishing at your feet

This brown trout was taken on a dry fly on the Red Deer River, Alberta.

works best in autumn. It also helps to fish areas that are lit by sunlight, particularly along a bubble line. Trout are sight feeders and can spot a fly better under these circumstances. Where possible, try to cast in an upstream direction so you don't spook the fish, which will be facing upstream. When moving upstream, walk some distance back from the stream so you aren't silhouetted against the skyline—you don't want to startle the fish. Wear earth-coloured clothes; fish can see colours. Finally, point the tip of your rod down towards the fly at all times during the drift to reduce drag, and lift easy on a strike.

It's not just cutthroat trout that can be targeted by fly fishing at your feet. You can catch brook trout, brown trout, bull trout, Kokanee and rainbow trout using the same tactics. They are best taken with dry flies and streamers. Some of my favourite dry fly patterns are Brown Elk Hair Caddis, Goddard Caddis, Royal Wulff, Yellow and Royal Humpys, Blue-winged Olives, Yellow and Orange Stimulators, Parachute Adams, Yellow Turk's Tarantula and Letort Hoppers. Use sizes 12–16, smaller for bank-hugging cutthroats.

For streamers, a Muddler Minnow is a good bet and will often draw bull trout from their lair as well as scrappy cutties. Other good streamers for bank-hugging trout are the Clouser Minnow, Byford's Natural Zonker, Black Marabou Muddler and Black or Olive Woolhead Sculpins, all fished with a sinking tip fly line. Often, you'll need to add a split shot to your tippet (about 12 inches back from the streamer) to get it down into the strike zone when fishing in fast water.

Don't overlook the obvious when out fishing for trout during summer and autumn; try fishing at your feet. You won't be disappointed!

Pocket Water Pickings

If one-third of the fish in a stream are at the head of a typical well-defined pool in a foothills or mountain stream during summer, where are the rest? Many are no doubt in deep, more or less straight runs, but the vast majority are in pocket water.

Pocket water can best be described as those areas of microhabitat not directly associated with classic pools. Examples include reaches between pools with a variety of structures; areas between boulders, both submerged and exposed; areas downstream of boulders, and in and around boulder gardens, situated between pools; areas on the inside bend of streams, especially those with some large woody debris or better yet a log or logjam, or with some overhanging vegetation; areas in the form of small pools on the edge of streams associated with tiny tributaries; areas that form tiny backwaters below islands, especially those in the shade; and more or less indiscreet areas that are in shadows, up tight against a stream bank—I mean tight, within a foot or two. In other words, a whole lot of territory that many anglers walk right on by on their way to the heads of pools and/or deep runs. If you carefully fish pocket water, you'll be surprised at the size of some of the brutes that you'll catch.

To a trout, a foothills or mountain stream is a pretty impoverished place. Water temperatures are generally cool, if not downright cold, but after all, trout are a cold water species of fish. However, cold temperatures limit photosynthetic activity—the primary building block in the food web—and this limits production of aquatic invertebrates. Food supplies are meagre in even the most productive streams due to the torrential nature of stream flows in both foothills and mountain streams in Alberta and British Columbia. When a food item floats on by, a trout had better grab it. The trouble is, most of the invertebrate drift takes place at night (see page 57). Being sight feeders, trout no doubt miss out on some fine dining opportunities because they can't see their prey when it's dark.

Trout lairs are located near the large boulders on the right-hand side of this photo.

What does this tell you? That trout in pocket water are easy pickings if you know when and how to fly fish these spots, despite the turbulent water and tricky currents that drag a fly immediately. I like fishing pocket water. You follow a strategy whereby you fish literally all of the potential areas of trout microhabitat by breaking it down into an imaginary grid. And you'll be surprised at the results.

Learn to read the water: Always keep a keen eye open for good holding water. It requires a lot of experience to understand the best places where fish will be found.

For starters, you should fish with a lightweight fly rod, 4- to 6-weight being best, and use a floating line—weight forward—with a tapered leader and short tippet. I prefer a short tippet when fishing pocket water in small streams because pinpoint casting is necessary; I'm often targeting a small target area, 25–50 feet distant.

You'll need to wear felt-soled wading boots because mountain streams can be swift flowing and have rounded rocks, boulders and cobble. You'll break some bones if you aren't careful, even with felt-soled wading boots. Wear a wading belt, in case you do go in the drink. I prefer to use breathable waders because they're comfortable, especially on a hot day. Streams in the foothills and mountains are cool at best and often downright cold at worst, but neoprene waders are just too hot during summer.

Dress in earth colours, and wear polarized sunglasses and a baseball cap.

On a hot day you can get by with shorts. If possible, dress in earth colours to break your silhouette and make it more difficult for trout to spot you and spook. By all means get yourself some polarized sunglasses; they eliminate glare and will help you see the stream bottom when you're wading, so that you know where to put your feet. A baseball cap with a long brim is also an asset to shade your eyes. Don't forget the sunscreen, and some insect repellent can also come in handy to ward off pesky flies and mosquitoes.

Dry flies are generally the ticket when fishing pocket water in small streams, and there are many to choose from. I prefer to fish pocket water with various dry flies with white wings, which are highly visible. A Royal or Green Humpy, Irresistible Wulff, Royal Coachman, Parachute Adams, Turk's Tarantula and Royal Wulff all have white wings that are just large enough to make them noticeable in mountain streams. This is no joking matter because you'll have to pick out these flies in areas of bright sun, shadow, along bubble lines and dancing among boulders. Even if you have perfect vision, seeing your fly in the water will be a challenge.

Lots of other flies are deadly. For example, an olive, orange or royal Stimulator is a great dry fly to fish pocket water, if not one of the best. An Adam's Humpy or Trude Humpy work well, although they're a bit harder to spot. The various mayfly spinners are more suitable for pools than pocket water but are a good bet for mountain streams. Any number of caddis dry flies work well, starting with a tan Elk Hair Caddis or a Deer Hair Caddis. Elk hair and deer hair are very buoyant. They make good caddis fly patterns that tend to float high, are visible and catch a lot of trout. A Deer Hair Caddis and a grey Caddis Cripple will also get lots of strikes. Try to match your fly to the hatch. Look for adult insects on stream side vegetation, floating on the surface, flying about or crawling on boulders.

Use dry flies to target rainbow trout in pocket water.

Check out the pocket water in the left corner of this photo near the boulders.

As a rule, a large fly will catch just as many trout in pocket water as a small one, if not more. In fact, I prefer larger sizes of dry flies—for example, a 10 rather than a 14–16—if I'm fishing a small mountain stream. On a large stream, I'd go to a smaller pattern. When a dry fly hits pocket water, a nearby trout usually strikes out of instinct as much as anything as the fly drifts on by. It has only a spit second to rise and try to swallow its suspected prey. It's harder for a trout to see a small fly in turbulent pocket water, and for this reason my choice is a size 10–12 in most situations.

When you arrive at a stream and are deciding where to go fishing, spend a few moments analyzing the situation. There will no doubt be all manner of fish habitat in front of you. Break the stream down in your mind into "fishable" sections in an imaginary grid. Cast upstream, and begin by fishing from the stream bank, working the near-shore inside bank area. When I

say "near-shore," I mean within a foot of two of the stream bank. Short casts work best. Drop your fly carefully, by means of a dump cast. Aim high, overpower the cast and stop the rod sharply. There should be a momentary drag-free float. You don't want to spook a skittish trout by tossing your line over top of it. Work from the near side stream bank to the centre of the stream, out towards the far bank, mending your line as you go. Don't forget to strip, strip, strip while your line drifts in the current because you don't want any slack line. When a pocket water trout strikes, it hits fast. Hook-ups must be quick.

Take three to four casts in each section in your imaginary grid before moving on to areas that haven't been fished. Pick your spots carefully as you go along. Pay particular attention to boulder gardens and other areas of microhabitat that I mentioned earlier on. You may have to do some wading to reach the far side of the stream. If you don't get any action, make your way upstream. My guess is that you will get some action if you don't hurry and are careful with your casts. Use dry fly dressing often to ensure that your fly floats high at all times, and freshen it up occasionally.

If a trout rises but misses the fly, try again. It will often take it the second or third time around. If you hook it and it gets off, give it rest before you try to catch it again. Use a different pattern the next time that you try to catch it, however. Don't be surprised if you catch it the second time around because the chances are good that it will strike again. In fact, even if you spook a trout when you're wading, come back and try to catch it later. Trout are territorial, and it won't be far off. It will often take a well-presented fly if it is given a break.

Use nymphs and streamers on the way back downstream to mop up if you're looking for some different kind of action, or if you are fishing an area with an undercut bank to draw trout from their lair. You'll need to switch to a floating line with

a sinking tip in these cases. Cast upstream, tight along the undercut bank, and mend the line sharply downstream. This will cause the fly to "swim" downstream, parallel to the bank, often with a trout in hot pursuit. You'll catch the odd mountain whitefish using nymphs, and don't be surprised if you hook-up an occasional bull trout when using streamers. A good bet is always a Muddler Minnow, which can be fished either dry or wet for bull trout. Cutthroats are not averse to rising for this pattern either. A bead head Hares Ear or a Prince Nymph will do the trick on mountain whitefish.

Pocket water in mountain streams should be fished throughout the summer months and on into September and early October, from early morning to the evening for best results. Forget getting up at daybreak. It isn't necessary. The bite is best during the daytime. Fishing pocket water is a whole new world for some fly fishers, but it's a lot of fun and a challenge worth taking. And you'll be surprised at the number of trout that you'll catch and the fun you'll have doing it.

Most trout will take a well-presented fly.

Fly Fishing from Drift Boats and Rafts

If you want to experience some red-hot fly fishing action on trout streams, one of the best ways is to fish from a Mackenzie-style drift boat or an inflatable rubber raft. I've been on many guided float trips on drift boats and rafts in Alberta and British Columbia, so I speak from experience about how good the fishing can be using these types of boats.

In both drift boats and rafts, the oarsman faces downstream, rowing and steering to position them in the current. The sports sit in the bow and stern, also facing downstream. The best casting position is up front, where the sport can see everything ahead of him and cast accurately if he knows what he's doing. The sport in the back is at a wee bit of a disadvantage because he can't see ahead quite as well and is restricted in terms of where he can cast. It's probably a good idea for the sports to switch stations once in a while to be fair to each other.

The sport in the stern has to keep an eye out for his partner up front and wait for him to cast first to minimize line tangles, which are inevitable regardless of whether you're fishing from a raft or drift boat because of unanticipated casts. Drift boats have a minimum of encumbrances to snag your fly line. Rafts have more encumbrances, and because you're often seated while casting, you'll encounter more snags as a consequence of your low casting profile. Be careful not to hook the oarsman, especially when fishing with streamers.

When fly fishing from a drift boat or raft, you normally cast downstream—not upstream, the conventional way to fly fish on a stream. When you have made a downstream cast, you must mend your line (upstream) once, twice or as often as necessary to maintain a natural, drag-free drift. A standard, straight-line cast is used most often whether in the bow or stern in a raft or drift boat. The other types of cast used frequently are the reach cast, followed by a roll cast. For the sport at the stern of the boat, the sideways cast is an asset.

Modern rafts ride high in the water and are ideal for shallow streams.

The sport in the front of a raft or drift boat has the best station when fly fishing.

You'll make a lot of casts during the day, and unless you manage your casts you'll come down with a case of tennis elbow. Minimize your false casts. Pick up the fly line by using roll casts, or use Belgian casts when necessary for casting large, heavy streamers or casting into the wind.

Strip some extra line so that you're always ready for a strike and can play out some extra line if you hook a large fish. Keep the tip of your rod pointed at the fly. Don't be afraid to dance dry flies, particularly in attractor patterns: twist your rod tip in a corkscrew motion and watch the fly literally dance on the water. Another way to drive trout nuts is by twitching the fly using short strips, which almost always gets a rise out of aggressive fish.

Don't try to bring a fish to reel until you have it under control—that first few seconds after a hook set is critical in landing trout on barbless hooks, in particular, so play the fish with your hand on the fly line at the start until you have it under control, then bring it to reel.

It's easy to land a small trout from either drift boats or rafts, and in most cases you should be able to release small trout on your own. If you are using barbless hooks, you shouldn't have to take the fish out of the water; just twist the hook to dislodge it. Always carry haemostats for the occasional fish that's badly hooked. Many times the guide will be otherwise occupied with maneuvring the boat and won't be able to provide any assistance, so you're expected to take care of yourself.

If you hook a large trout, however, the guide will usually beach the boat so that you can disembark and try to land it from shore. In my experience, it's a lot easier to land a large fish from shore rather than from a raft or drift boat. You'll need a landing net for big trout. The trick is to carefully "lift" them off the stream bottom so that you or the guide can get a landing net under them. This is easier said than done—many a large trout has been lost at this critical moment. I can't emphasize the importance of a firm, steady hand when landing a large trout. Don't "horse" them, or you'll break the tippet!

A Mackenzie-style drift boat can be used to get to difficult-to-reach fishing spots.

What to Bring

Fly rods and reels (4- to 6-weight for dry fly fishing; 7- to 8-weight for nymphs or streamers); always bring at least one spare rod and reel packed in a sturdy case in case of breakages. Leaders; bring three each of 9-foot, 0X and 3X. Check with your guide to see whether flies are supplied. And bring a landing net in case of hooking a large fish.

It's wise to bring a few other things as well:

• a dry pack or water-repellent day pack with a change of clothes and extra socks

• rain gear and a windbreaker or warm jacket, depending on the time of year

• a hat and polarized sunglasses

• chest waders (breathable or neoprene depending on the time of the year) and felt-soled wading shoes

• fingerless wool gloves for spring and autumn trips

• sunscreen and insect repellent.

If you're prepared, chances are you'll have a great trip, regardless of whether the fish are biting.

Conventional rubber rafts are functional but challenging to cast from.

Chapter 4

The Fish: Six Fly Fishing Target Species

*If I fished only to capture fish, my fishing trips would have
ended long ago.*

—Zane Grey

Fly Fishing for Arctic Grayling

Both Yukon and the Northwest Territories
are hotbeds for the fly fisher's dream fish:
Arctic grayling. This quintessential fish is
also fairly common in northern British
Columbia, Alberta, Saskatchewan, Manitoba and much of western Nunavut.

An Arctic grayling from the Stark River, NWT.

*Sadly, Alberta's range of Arctic
grayling has been shrinking as
a result of habitat destruction,
dewatering of streams (resulting in
rises in stream temperature), block-
ages of movement due to barriers
such as improperly installed cul-
verts and over fishing. Grayling are
also sensitive to siltation and sedi-
mentation from improper road con-
struction as a result of oil and gas
exploration and forestry operations
in Alberta's boreal forest has signifi-
cantly impacted their populations.*

*Alberta's subpopulations are esti-
mated to have declined predomi-
nantly in the 1950s to 1970s,
with 50 percent of subpopulations declining over 90 percent in
abundance. Yikes! These declines
represent a range contraction of
approximately 40 percent of their
historical range in Alberta according
to a report entitled "Status of the
Arctic grayling (Thymallus arti-
cus) in Alberta," written by Jordan
Walker in 2005.*

Adults migrate from ice-covered lakes and large rivers to small gravel or rock-bottomed tributaries during the spring breakup. Adult males are territorial on spawning grounds and will chase intruding small males. No nest is built; the eggs are simply broadcast over rocks and gravel. After spawning, adults return to their summer, autumn and winter homes in lakes or rivers.

Grayling inhabit clear waters of large, cold streams and lakes in shallow water less than 10–12 feet deep. Adults feed on a variety of invertebrates: aquatic insects such as mayflies, caddis flies and midges, and terrestrial insects such as bees, wasps, grasshoppers, ants and beetles. They also feed on small quantities of fish, fish eggs and even lemmings. Food studies on northern lakes indicate that terrestrial insects form the most important summer food of grayling, often comprising over half of their diet. Grayling are opportunistic feeders.

They tend to school, so when you catch one, others will often be nearby. They are also fond of outlet streams from large lakes, especially near the mouth. These are highly productive areas and have a large quantity of aquatic insects, especially filter feeding black fly larvae, which often literally blanket the streambed.

Catching Arctic grayling is not necessarily a slam dunk. The itinerant fly fisher had best be prepared for this eventuality and be versatile in their fly fishing approach. At times you'll have to go through your fly box before you select the right fly; there are no sure-fire, go-to flies that I've discovered despite many years of fishing for this peacock of the ichthyological world.

Arctic grayling inhabit cold, clear, shallow water in northern Canada.

Be prepared to search out grayling using dry flies, nymphs and streamers.

The best fly fishing for grayling is during summer and into autumn, when it can really heat up as the fish gorge themselves in preparation for a long winter. The good news is that Arctic grayling are usually cooperative from spring until autumn. However, they can be hard to locate during their spring spawning season due to their migratory nature.

When you're fly fishing in streams, be prepared to search out grayling using dry flies, nymphs and streamers, and have the rod and fly lines to suit such flies. This is especially the case when you're fishing remote areas in the north. Plan for contingencies because you won't know what you're up against until you hit the water, and conditions can be highly variable. Streams may be pushing more water than normal due to runoff and thunderstorms, or they may be only a trickle of their normal flows. Cold fronts might move in and put a halt to insect hatches, or high winds may arise and make casting a nightmare. Insect hatches are often sporadic throughout the range of grayling in northern Canada; it's unwise to count on ideal dry fly fishing conditions.

If you're after trophy fish, use a sink tip line with a 3-foot leader and tie on a streamer pattern. It's seldom necessary to fish with fluorocarbon because most streams are stained with tannins and lignin from muskeg, which imparts a brown tinge to the water. Grayling, especially large, dominant adults, are predacious fish and will attack most streamers with a vengeance. Fish streamers in the usual way: start by casting across and down runs and pools. Let the fly swing in a dead drift, twitching it from time to time to make it porpoise. Keep the line between your index and middle fingers to detect strikes, and then set the hook. Take a few steps downstream and repeat the process. You may want to switch to a 7- to 8-weight fly rod to improve your casting range if you're fishing heavy streamers in a large river. I've had good results with weighted black and olive Woolly Buggers, brown and purple cone-head Woolly Buggers and Marabou Muddler patterns. Natural patterns are the most consistent producers, not colourful, psychedelic streamers.

Should you be interested in just catching grayling, then bead head nymphs such as the Prince Nymph and Pheasant Tail are old standbys. Use a tapered leader with or without a strike indicator and fish the nymph in a dead drift. A strike indicator will help you see approximately where the fly is drifting. Nymphs can be effective when insect surface activity is slow or perhaps if grayling are in swift water. If grayling are turned off dry flies because they've been lined too often, switch to nymphs to get back in the game. Don't laugh; this sometimes happens out of northern lodges because guides tend to take clients to the same waters again and again. Check with locals regarding go-to nymphs. For example, in some Alberta foothill streams, the Rat Tail Special is often a choice wet fly when other patterns don't pan out.

If you're a diehard dry fly enthusiast, you may be disappointed in pursuit of your quarry because insect hatches are sporadic where grayling are found, plus fly patterns are rather limited compared with more southern standards. Two flies of choice are the venerable Elk Hair Caddis and Goddard Caddis because caddis flies are by far the most abundant insect in northern Canadian waters inhabited by grayling. My next choice would probably be a Brown or Grey Wulff, good imitations of the often abundant midges in grayling water, or perhaps a Black Gnat, which imitates black flies.

Often the best flies for grayling are foam fly attractor patterns in various colours: Turk's Tarantula, Madame X or Chernobyl Ant patterns. I'm not sure how long the foam fly fad will last, but for now they're

Go-to attractor patterns for grayling are foam flies that imitate adult stoneflies.

my go-to pattern when I first gear up, and they can be fished all day long, regardless of whether there's a hatch underway. They work well under all weather conditions. Stock up on these foam flies and fish them with a tapered leader and a floating line. The large, gaudy patterns are usually dynamite on grayling when fished in a dead drift or skated across holding water. They can be every bit as good as the Elk Hair or Goddard Caddis and Brown and Grey Wulff patterns or Black Gnats, often better because they're easier to see under poor light.

Sight cast to rising grayling or fish dry flies using a dead drift in promising holding water, mending your line as often as necessary. Don't be surprised if you can't spot any rising grayling. In terms of the size of flies, smaller is usually better even in lightly fished lakes and streams, with the exception of foam flies and streamers, where large flies are okay. If the grayling are off the usual patterns, go small—down to at least size 18.

> *Put it on their nose: Drop your fly on the exact spot where you've seen a rising fish or where you think one might be located. Precise, pinpoint casts are key to being successful.*

Keep your false casts to a minimum so as not to put Arctic grayling down; they line easily. They're wary of intruders in their pristine habitat and can see extremely well in their often clear water environs. Don't wade into a lake or stream any more than necessary. Stand back from the edge of the water; try to wear earth-coloured clothes; keep a fairly low profile, or you'll scare them.

> *Some fly patterns will almost consistently get strikes. Dry flies: Black Gnat, Elk Hair Caddis, Goddard Caddis, Brown or Grey Wulff, Royal Wulff, Red or Orange Humpys, Red or Yellow Stimulators, Black Ants. Streamers: Woolly Buggers and Marabou Muddlers. Wet flies: Stone Nymph, Black Gnat; bead head Prince Nymph and Gold Ribbed Hare's Ear searching nymphs.*

> *Use a size 12–16 dry/wet fly with a 9- to 12-foot leader with a short 4X tippet on a floating or sink tip fly line, and size 6–14 streamers, on a 4- to 6-weight fly rod to catch grayling.*

What about fly fishing for grayling in lakes? The good news is that what works in streams also works in lakes. The only disclaimer is that if grayling are rising and you can't see any insects on the water, the fish are probably after emergers. The Klinkhåmmer Special, or Klinkhammer, is a good choice under these circumstances because of the prevalance of caddis flies in grayling waters. Typically, grayling cruise the shallows of lakes in search of something to eat. If you're fishing from a boat, you can sight cast to cruising fish if you don't see any fish rising for flies. It usually isn't necessary to troll flies in lakes to get into some action, but if you can't locate a pod, keep this tactic in mind. Some of the best fishing in lakes is found near the mouths of inlet streams, where grayling congregate to capitalize on invertebrate drift that enters the still water. About the only thing that will scare them away from such areas is the sudden appearance of a lake trout with intentions of making a meal of the local grayling.

Photo Ops—When you land a grayling and want to capture the special moment with a photo, take heed of the following advice. Grayling tend to be slippery and can be hard to hold. First, wet your hands. Then remove the fish from the water and rest it in the palm of your hand. Gently raise its dorsal fin by grasping it between the index finger and thumb of your free hand. Put a smile on your face to record the moment. Have the photographer set the fill flash on the camera in the on position beforehand, to minimize shadow under a peaked hat. This is the signature picture that caps the joy of fly fishing for grayling. Savour the moment. Take a few photos just to make sure you get the image you want for your scrapbook, then gently release the fish to be caught another day.

Enigmatic Brook Trout

This section is about fly fishing for brook trout in still waters, where my experience includes Alberta, Labrador and Quebec. These places seem a world apart when it comes to flies as well as fly fishing techniques for trying to catch what is at times a rather enigmatic species, native to eastern North America. Populations in Alberta and British Columbia originated from stockings.

John Huff is a noted Canadian fishing guide, three-time captain and eight-time team member of the Canadian Fly Fishing Team. Being able to spend some time under his wing was a decided attraction in my choice of the Kenauk Reserve in Quebec, where we fished for brook trout with a wide selection of dry and wet flies and streamers (for more on my trip to Kenauk, see page 170). Some of his recommended patterns were typical still-water flies such as damselfly nymphs, Woolly Buggers (black and olive) and the Egg Sucking Leech; the Muddler Minnow streamer fly; dry flies such as the Adam's and Royal Wulff; and

Rest the fish in the palm of your hand and gently raise its dorsal fin for a photo.

The Hornberg Special, a Quebec fly, is a go-to pattern for brook trout.

the San Juan Worm, a searching nymph. Strangely, he did not single out the Hornberg streamer, which is an old-fashioned Quebec fly. When I asked Huff why, he said that it was a good fly for brook trout and it would work in the Kenauk, but other patterns seemed to be better producers. I did try a Hornberg streamer—a good fly for brook trout in western Canada's still waters—and quickly caught several fish. All of these flies will work in lakes with brook trout in the boreal forest and foothills, but not necessarily clear mountain lakes.

"I would describe brook trout as the most fickle of the trout and char species," said Huff. "They turn off and on, and it can be difficult to relate this behaviour to a particular weather, atmospheric or other condition. Some of the tactics I use when the fishing is tough are to use two or three flies—for example, a streamer and a couple of nymphs. Some of my favourites would be a Muddler Minnow, Bow River Bugger, Magog Smelt, Dragon Fly Nymph, GRHE

bead head and the Prince Nymph. When they are up top on dries, sometimes matching the hatch isn't the answer. Try a similar pattern that is two or three times bigger than the naturals, or a commotion fly like a Bow River Bugger. Try the unusual, unorthodox or obnoxious; you never know what might work."

Huff's strategy for fishing brook trout is pretty straightforward: work shoreline structures (i.e., submerged logs, weed beds, boulders and rock outcrops), islands, bays and points with short, straight-line casts. Strip, strip, strip when fishing with wet flies and streamers. Strip, pause, strip, pause...cast again, and repeat the process. Don't false cast more than you have to. Pause on your back cast while you get your target in the crosshairs, accelerate on the forward cast and then gently drop your fly when the tip of your rod is level with the horizon. For dry flies, use short straight-line casts, gently drop the fly, twitch it from time to time and get ready for a strike.

An eastern brook trout taken from Awesome Lake in Labrador.

Change your trajectory and use a chop cast if the wind comes up. The short casts improve the odds of more and better hook-ups—too much line out makes for hard hook-ups and more lost trout. The action (stripping and/or twitching) gets the attention of fish, which often barrel towards the presentation. Pay attention for hits with wet flies and streamers by keeping contact with your line, and keep your eye on dry patterns for rises. Don't yank the hook on rises. Wait for the fish to take the fly. Huff's no-nonsense fly fishing techniques pay dividends, and at the end of the day you should still have some steam left over for day two on the water.

In spring and autumn, brook trout will be found in the shallows, but during the heat of summer, you have to switch to a full sink line if you expect any action, and work the usual streamers. Do a slow troll or let the boat drift in the wind and rip the line from time to time to entice neutral fish to strike.

Longer is better (at least 12 feet) when it comes to leaders in the often crystal clear waters of Maligne Lake. Use a fast-sinking fly line. Colourful streamers are recommended by just about everybody who fishes Maligne Lake: Doc Spratley, Mickey Finn, Little Brook Trout and Little Rainbow Trout, along with Full Back Mayfly Nymphs and Double Shrimp. The Magog Smelt is a colourful Atlantic salmon streamer that just might entice some action on finicky brook trout in places like Maligne Lake. A Gold Ribbed Hare's Ear (GRHE) is probably the most popular of the impressionistic nymphs. It can be tied large or small, light or dark, and can imitate anything from a small mayfly nymph to a large stonefly nymph.

Blind casts are generally a waste of time. Usually, you have to troll fairly fast during the open water fishing season, cover a lot of ground and hope to bump into some fish. Let out enough line to get down 20–30 feet (into the strike zone) and rip the line forward as often as possible. While it's not the only way to catch brook trout in Maligne Lake, it's one of the better techniques. Troll, troll and troll some more.

On the other side of the border from Jasper National Park lies Fortress Lake, British Columbia's premier lake for brook trout—one of the best in North America—in Hamber Provincial Park, where fishing techniques are just a bit different. Alberta fly fishing authority Phillip Rowley shared his knowledge with me about fly fishing for brook trout in this unspoiled lake. Rowley said, "Although there is evidence of [trout] feeding on dragonflies and scuds, the prominent food base—especially for the larger trout—are their younger brothers. Brook trout are opportunistic, and in this case cannibalistic…they're the sole inhabitants, and there are no other fish present.

They're looking for the big fish, being the top predator. Give them something that's worth their while! We found leeches and big bait fish patterns worked best," he said, "like big brown Woolly Buggers, Clouser Minnow and White Rabbit Leech. They weren't too selective on size or colour." The same situation applied when I fished for brook trout in Awesome Lake in Labrador.

Rowley also suggested looking for structures that will draw trout. "In Fortress Lake, there's a lot of sunken debris caused by avalanches sweeping fallen timber into the lake. Fish congregate around these spots, and around points near drop-offs. Creek mouths are always a draw too, because food tumbles out of streams. For the most part, we used clear intermediate lines—the Stillwater kinds—or moved the boat upwind in some areas, cut the power

A brook trout from Maligne Lake, Alberta.

Big brookies from Fortress Lake, British Columbia.

and let it drift. Sometimes we'd just blind cast. In some areas the water was so clear we could see the trout, and then we would use Type VI lines because they would be cruising 10–15 feet down. They'd quickly dash after the fly and eat it."

Brook trout fishing picks up in autumn as water temperatures drop to their preferred range of 7–16° C. This explains why fishing for brook trout is often slow in popular lakes such as Spruce Coulee Reservoir in Alberta's Cypress Hills Provincial Park until October, when it can be red hot. According to Scott and Crossman's textbook *Freshwater Fishes of Canada* (1973), brook trout tend to seek temperatures below 20° C when surface waters warm up. Pack your thermometer, check surface water temperatures and adjust your fishing strategy accordingly.

Why is there such a disparity in brook trout flies and fly fishing techniques? In a nutshell, it comes down to variations in food, still-water habitat and structure, and the need to adapt flies and fishing techniques to suit the circumstances. Brook trout are carnivorous and will eat almost anything they can swallow. Small fish are targeted where they're available, which is one reason why streamers are often dynamite.

Goldeye Galore

While the bull trout is Alberta's official fish emblem, the goldeye would have to be Alberta's people's fish: folks in several Alberta cities, including Medicine Hat, Lethbridge, Edmonton and Red Deer, can catch them in the city limits on the banks of their respective rivers. Goldeye are often found right in many Albertans' very own backyards, although they may not be there throughout the whole year because of their migratory behaviour. Goldeye are also present in Saskatchewan and Manitoba and in isolated pockets in Ontario and the Northwest Territories. In Manitoba, popular rivers include the Assiniboine, Red, Saskatchewan and Winnipeg rivers. And in

Goldeye have large yellow eyes.

Saskatchewan, the top locations are the South and North Saskatchewan rivers.

Goldeye are one of Alberta's more abundant fish species, and also one of the most unheralded. They're present in all the major rivers in Alberta from south to north: South Saskatchewan, Oldman, Lower Bow, Red Deer, North Saskatchewan, Athabasca, Peace and Slave rivers, with inroads in the Smoky and Wabasca rivers. Despite their widespread distribution and relative abundance, seasonally, they're relatively unknown as a game fish, and Alberta's anglers are poorer because of this lack of notoriety.

It's been my good fortune to fish for goldeye in virtually all of Alberta's major rivers—you name it, I've probably been there, done that. In fact, I enjoy catching them so much that I geared up for goldeye instead of walleye when I had an opportunity to catch them in the Mikkwa River (a tributary to the Peace River) many years ago.

Why are goldeye so much fun to catch? For starters, you don't have to be an expert angler to catch goldeye. Second, you don't need a lot of fancy gear. For flies, there are lots of old standbys: grasshopper patterns, small nymphs and streamers are among my favourites. Third, they're forgiving—if you miss one, don't worry; another one will probably take your fly, often on the same cast. Get the drift?

Goldeye are generally found in large rivers with turbid water, and a light-coloured fly stands out in stark contrast under such conditions. A wide range of attractor patterns are excellent choices. Goldeye are often found throughout pools but are usually at the top end. They often frequent the mouths of clear-running streams where they enter large, silty rivers. I've had some of my best fishing for goldeye at the mouths of the St. Mary and Belly rivers where they enter the Oldman River upstream of Lethbridge, which are prime locations during

Attractor patterns are ideal for locating goldeye in large streams and rivers.

late spring and early summer. Pick any size-able tributary stream to the large home waters of goldeye in Alberta, and you'll likely have similar success.

Goldeye are a sleek, silver-coloured fish. They are predacious and have sharp teeth. Their eyes are set near the top of their head so they can see above them in silty water. In Alberta, the largest goldeye would be about 20 inches in length, with the provincial record weighing 4.125 pounds, taken by R. Weber in the Battle River Dam in 1974. According to *The Fishes of Alberta* (1992) by Nelson and Paetz, it's possible that a world record goldeye was taken in the Bow River below the Bassano Dam on June 24, 1967—after the gills and entrails were removed, it weighed 4 pounds. Their diet consists mainly of water beetles, midges and various aquatic insects. Nelson and Paetz reported, "The diet seems to reflect the size of the fish and availability of food items. Goldeye also feed on other fish and occasionally consume aquatic tetra-pods (e.g., shrews)." They are renowned for their lengthy migrations, and one goldeye

was reported to have travelled some 2000 kilometres (1240 miles) in 15 days. They're spring spawners, and females lay semi-buoyant eggs that drift downstream in large rivers before hatching. The oldest Alberta goldeye was thought to be about 13 years old.

Understandably, many anglers mis-take mooneye for goldeye. Probably the best way to differentiate them is by their eyes. Goldeye have large yellow eyes, whereas only the very top of the iris is golden in a moon-eye, while the bottom is silver (i.e., they have a "half-moon" of gold at the top of the eye). Another distin-guishing characteristic relates to the front of the dorsal fin, which is parallel or slightly behind the origin of the anal fin in a gold-eye, whereas the dorsal fin origin is in front of the anal fin origin in a mooneye. Otherwise they're quite similar in appearance, with later-ally compressed, silver bodies and large scales.

The top of the iris is golden in a mooneye, but the bottom is silver.

When fishing for goldeye, my choice is a 4-weight fly rod with matching line weight—you don't really need a tapered leader and can get by with a 9-foot matching monofilament leader, no problem. While I'm a big fan of foam flies such as the Chernobyl Ant, Madame X or Turk's Tarantula, most hopper patterns will also do the trick, as will various searching nymphs such as a Pheasant Tail or Prince Nymph, the latter flies fished with a strike indicator.

One of the first things you'll notice when you hook a goldeye is that they're hard to handle as they pirouette through the water, trying to dislodge the hook. It's not uncommon for them to put on a bit of a display of acrobatics in the process. They're underrated as a game fish and deserve more credit for their sporting qualities, which are comparable to trout and whitefish of a similar size. As a bonus, in Alberta the limit on goldeye (and mooneye) is 10, there's no size limit, seasons are long and they're cosmopolitan in distribution, often found in or near Alberta's major urban centres—now you know why I maintain they're a fish of the people.

Goldeye are considered a delicacy when smoked, and the name "Winnipeg Goldeye" conjures up all sorts of images of fine dining on the Canadian Pacific Railway, where they were a featured item on the menu for many years.

Late Season Lake Trout

Just when a lot of fishermen are putting away their gear for the year, lake trout fishing is hitting high gear. And perhaps that's the reason why a lot of fishermen miss out on some of the best fly fishing to be had for lake trout throughout their range in Canada. As surface water temperatures cool to 10° C, or thereabouts, lake trout once again find their preferred water temperature in relatively shallow littoral zones, and action picks up as they move inshore from their summer quarters in the deepest part of a lake to spawn and to feed.

Lake trout are autumn spawners and home in on windswept, shallow shoals and reefs in anticipation of the annual

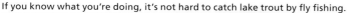

If you know what you're doing, it's not hard to catch lake trout by fly fishing.

spawning season. The exact spawning date is affected by factors such as latitude, the weather leading up to the spawning period as well as the size and topography of a lake, but it can start as early as September in Yukon, Northwest Territories and Nunavut, through to October and into November farther south in Canada, on the southern edge of their range. Adults may also spawn in tributary streams of some lakes. The spawning act itself occurs during the middle of the night, and prior to the spawn, adult lake trout stage near key spawning areas. During late summer and early autumn, lake trout also feed actively to beef up in preparation for a long, cold winter; consequently, action is often red hot at this time of year.

While it's often difficult to pinpoint actual spawning beds on large lakes, many such areas feature bottoms of large boulders and rubble in relatively shallow water, anywhere from 1 to 40 feet deep, often on the windswept side of islands and shorelines,

Lake trout move to shallow water to spawn in autumn, a great time for fly anglers to catch them.

or associated with mid-water, relatively shallow reefs. Typically, these spots show as light yellow in colour on sunny, late summer and autumn days. There's evidence that lake trout head to the same spawning locations year after year, which may be marked by their tails when they use them to clear rubble and boulders on such reefs of sediment prior to actually spawning. Many a veteran fishing guide has plotted such locations with GPS coordinates or they have these spots stored in the back of their minds because they're consistent producers of adult lake trout.

Because lake trout are large fish, it's necessary to use an 8- or 9-weight, medium action fly rod that's capable of landing fish up to at least 35 pounds. A medium action rod is better than a fast or slow action rod for pitching large streamers. Use a sink tip line and 20-pound test monofilament leader, cut in a 3-foot length. Short leaders will turn large flies over better than long leaders; they'll also get a fly into the strike zone quickly. It isn't necessary to use stainless steel swivels or wire leaders when fly fishing for lake trout; simply tie the fly onto the monofilament leader with a clinch knot. A large-arbour reel is a definite asset when trying to land a large trout. These reels take line in that much faster than a medium- or small-arbour reel because of their improved rate of retrieve; each revolution of the spool retrieves more line than the smaller reels.

Streamers are the ticket for lake trout: large deceivers, zonkers and cone heads with enough weight to quickly drop into several feet of water, at least. Generally, larger is better, and I'd suggest a size 2 up to 4, with a razor sharp hook tip because lake trout have hard jaws and mouths. Touch up the hook tip with a handheld sharpening stone, especially on stainless steel hooks, which are not usually razor sharp when they're manufactured and need periodic sharpening. Use natural patterns that imitate bait fish such as the cisco, a species of

Lake trout deceiver fly patterns.

the whitefish family that is a favourite prey species. While many different colours will entice strikes, my favourite colours are white, yellow and orange, all of which are good producers. If the action on these colours drops off, then switch to more natural olive, purple or black. An orange cone-head Woolly Bugger pattern is usually a good producer, followed by a white rabbit-strip zonker. Some other commercial flies that I fancy are black and olive Slimy Sculpins or the Mickey Finn, and a red and white Pixies Revenge.

Once you've zeroed in on prime lake trout lairs, start by fan casting in a grid if winds are relatively calm. Let the fly sink to the bottom or near bottom before starting your retrieve, stripping the line during the retrieve. Should you actually spot a cruising lake trout, by all means switch to sight casting, targeting the area in front of or beside the trout. If there's a chop on the water, you can use the wind drift to troll over productive water, or simply troll using an outboard motor at a slow speed. Slower is better when trolling; try doing some figure-eight patterns to cover offshore spawning beds, paying particular attention on the turn because that's often when you'll get a strike. Be sure to power strip the line from time to time when trolling to entice passive fish. Be patient—the trout aren't everywhere, so you'll have to search them out. On another note, an old trick is to cast behind a hooked trout when fishing with a buddy, which often pays dividends because lake trout tend to travel in small schools. One hooked fish may attract the attention of another lake trout, and the straggler will often charge a second streamer. If the bite drops off, there's a trick to get back into the action: change patterns and/or use a heavier fly to gain some extra depth. More often than not, if action slows you're not fishing in the strike zone, and you simply have to fish in a bit deeper water.

Lake trout tend to hit a fly hard, and in order to set the hook in their tough jaws

Large, colourful streamers are deadly on lake trout.

and mouths, it's necessary to yard on it with attitude, particularly when using barbless hooks, which is the law across most of Canada. Otherwise, the trout will shake its head and throw the hook. Very large lake trout tend to dog a lure and just won't move when first hooked. They'll simply remain suspended in the water column, hardly budging. At this juncture you should quickly try to reel in any slack line and attempt to bring the trout to reel as soon as possible. Don't try to land a large trout by handling the fly line or you'll end with a line burn, and in all likelihood you'll lose the fish. You'll have to be patient and carefully pump your rod to get the fish to make a move; be sure to set the drag midway, not too tight or you'll risk breaking the tip of your fly rod or snapping a knot. Then it's just a matter of playing the fish until it tires and can be netted. Follow the basics. When a trout runs give it some line; when it stops its run, slowly reel it in. Don't let the trout get underneath a boat or it may break your rod. Likewise, keep it away from the motor or your line may get tangled in the propeller.

In order to fully enjoy late-season action, ensure you're geared for some relatively cold weather because even on sunny days it can be crisp on the water. In fact, when the water temperature drops to 10° C, it can be downright cold at times because of the wind chill when you're travelling in an outboard motorboat from one point to another on a big lake. Dress in layers.

I've enjoyed some great late-season fly fishing for lake trout on Great Slave Lake out of Frontier Fishing Lodge and on Great Bear Lake out of Plummer's Arctic Lodges in the Northwest Territories during late August. Lake trout are stacked in the shallows in preparation for spawning on both these lakes in late August and early September. Fishing was so good that catches in excess of 20 big lake trout a day on Great Slave Lake were the norm. Compare this to Atlantic salmon fishing during the same time of the year when the hook-ups would be few and far between, and for Chinook salmon, where an angler might catch only one salmon during a week of hard fishing at some lodges, or get skunked. And now you know why I don't store my gear until I've had my way with lake trout on a fly rod. Oh, and don't forget the shore lunch—lake trout are delicious!

Contact Frontier Fishing Lodge or Plummer's Arctic Lodges for details regarding late-season lake trout fishing in the Northwest Territories. Check out the spectacular NWT Tourism website for vacation planning.

Mountain Whitefish on a Fly

They are never going to win a beauty contest, but it's really a shame that mountain whitefish get the short shrift when it comes to fly fishing—all the glory goes to members of the trout family when mountain whitefish should rate higher on the list.

Mountain whitefish are one of the most plentiful species of game fish in Alberta, found in all the major drainages: the Milk, Oldman, Bow, Red Deer, North Saskatchewan, Athabasca and Peace. For the most part, in Alberta they're confined to rivers and streams, although they're also found in some lakes. Mountain whitefish are also abundant throughout the entire province of British Columbia and many of the western states. They're relatively easy to catch if you know how and when to fish for them and can be taken with nymphs and wet flies or, rarely, dry flies.

Mountain whitefish are abundant and relatively easy to catch in mountain streams.

From late August until freeze-up, mountain whitefish gather in spawning aggregations. Spawning occurs from late September to early November over gravel. The eggs are broadcast. No redd is built. After spawning, they gravitate to overwintering pools, where they remain until the spring breakup. During autumn, you can get in all the fishing for mountain whitefish you want in just a few select pools; there's no need to travel very far in search of their hideouts. It's not that they can't be taken at other times of the year; it's just that autumn is the traditional time to catch mountain whitefish.

So, what should you do to search out congregations of mountain whitefish? Start by asking the locals a few questions if you're not familiar with a river. Mountain whitefish typically hole up in certain pools during autumn that are well known to local fishermen. As a kid growing up in the Crowsnest Pass, I used to know the best pools on the Crowsnest River by name: Tapay's hole, Marco's hole, etc. Look for the silver flash of whitefish as they jostle for position in the current. They're fairly easy to see with polarized sunglasses once you figure out what to look for. Take your time when scouting out a pool, and spend a few minutes on the lookout for mountain whitefish. They tend to move about a lot, and if you are patient you'll be able to spot them. Another way to search them out is to fish pools and runs by working your way downstream on unfamiliar waters and "sample" using a brown hackle fly as you go along. These fish tend to school, so when you catch one, expect others to be nearby.

Don't leave fish to find fish: This is a favourite saying of fishing guide Vic Bergman that means if you're onto fish, don't move on until they stop biting. It's a testament to the spotty distribution of trout in many freestone rivers and streams.

It's not uncommon to find several dozen and up to a hundred or more mountain whitefish in select pools during autumn. During summer, however, they are widely dispersed throughout streams and tend to favour turbulent pocket water, as well as deep runs and large pools. They are masters at inhabiting swift water; with their streamlined, torpedo-shaped body, they use their fins to suspend themselves in fast, turbulent water often just off the stream bottom.

Only a few weighted nymphs (a bead head Prince Nymph and Gold Ribbed Hare's Ear) and wet flies (a Royal Coachman and a Brown Hackle Peacock) are commonly used to catch mountain whitefish. All are fished by nymphing, generally using a sink tip fly line with a 9-foot, 4- to 6-weight fly rod. Because southern Alberta is subject to gusty winds, it can be an advantage at times to fish with a 5- or 6-weight rod. I find that a long rod provides better leverage and is an aid in making fast hook sets. Leaders can be in the 7.5- to 9-foot range.

Mountain whitefish don't seem to be leader or tippet shy, and 4X and 5X tippets will work fine in most nymph (or wet fly) fishing situations. I prefer to use a strike indicator with this rig. Mountain whitefish have keen eyesight and a tiny mouth; you can't go too small when choosing your flies—unless it's possible to fish them with bait, which is legal in certain streams and at certain times. In these cases, a larger fly will work. Generally, you should use a size 12–14 fly when fishing for mountain whitefish, although smaller sizes will also catch fish. Where the use of bait is permitted, locals tend to bait a Royal Coachman or a Brown Hackle Peacock with a maggot and fish with the maximum number of hooks permissible in open water.

It's a rare day when you'll catch a mountain whitefish on a dry fly. I've only done this a few times. They can be difficult to hook with a dry fly because their mouth is on the bottom of their head.

Target mountain whitefish with nymphs; note the nymph hooked in the jaw.

Fish for mountain whitefish by heading off in a downstream direction on streams because it's easier to cast nymphs and wet flies than when fishing upstream. Because mountain whitefish are hard to hook, I tend to use a reach cast where possible. Cast the fly upstream of the target area and mend the line in an upstream direction as it hits the water—mend once, twice or more often to create a longer, drag-free drift. Strip the line and keep the tip of the rod pointed towards the strike indicator. Don't be surprised if you get a few trout with this outfit, besides mountain whitefish.

Mountain whitefish are bottom feeders. Their natural diet is primarily larval aquatic insects: mayflies, stoneflies and caddis flies. While they will rise from a stream bottom, you'll catch more of them if you bounce nymphs and wet flies along the stream bottom. Expect to lose some tackle when you're fishing for mountain whitefish. If you don't, you're probably not fishing deep enough. Often, you'll have to add several spit shot about a foot back of your fly to get it into the strike zone. Mountain whitefish are delicate feeders. They don't strike hard, and you have to pay attention to detect a strike. When a fish bites, the strike indicator will disappear or move erratically.

When you do hook one, be ready for a tug of war; they tend to fight the good fight. Don't horse them, though, or you'll dislodge the hook—slow and steady is the best way to reel them in. They dive deep and rarely break the water. Don't play them to exhaustion if you don't plan to keep them because they can't tolerate a lot of stress—release them gently after you've dislodged the fly and hold them facing the current until they swim away on their own.

Expect to catch them in a wide range of sizes, up to a couple of pounds or more. Old mountain whitefish are not uncommon, and they can live for many years—

Mountain whitefish are bottom feeders; bounce nymphs along the stream bottom.

Small mountain whitefish are excellent when smoked.

a mountain whitefish 29 years of age was taken from Spray Lakes Reservoir near Canmore, Alberta. The current Alberta record for mountain whitefish weighed 5 pounds, 10.5 ounces and was taken in Gap Lake off the Bow River, near Canmore, in 1991. From what I recall, the record for mountain whitefish was being broken nearly every year in the 1980s. I've taken many mountain whitefish in the 2- to 3-pound range in several streams along the foothills of the eastern slopes.

And if you like the odd fish for the table, you don't have to feel guilty about taking some home; they are quite abundant throughout most of Alberta. They are popular as table fish and are excellent when smoked—particularly the smaller mountain whitefish. They are also popular as "canners," not unlike pickled herring. Their scales should be scraped off using a knife with a serrated edge before they are grilled or smoked. They may not be pretty, but they are a worthy game fish and challenging to catch on a fly.

Some of the more popular streams for mountain whitefish in Alberta are the Athabasca, North Saskatchewan, Red Deer, Bow, Highwood, Sheep, Oldman, Livingstone, Crowsnest, Castle, Waterton, Belly and St. Mary rivers, to name but a few. The Red Deer River below Dickson Dam is popular, as are several other tail-water fisheries, such as on the Oldman River downstream of the Oldman River Dam. Fishing picks up on the Athabasca River near Hinton and Jasper when the river drops in autumn and the load of glacial silt declines. I've seen some real whoppers in the Bow River in the section downstream of Calgary to Carseland. The Elk River, near Fernie, is renowned for its outstanding fishing for mountain whitefish, as is the outlet of Kootenay Lake near Balfour in British Columbia.

Chris Hanks with a trophy pike from Trout Rock Lodge, NWT.

Northern Pike on a Fly

"If I only had two colours for pike flies, I'd pick chartreuse and black," Chris Hanks, my fishing guide, said emphatically. Chris and I were exploring Moose Bay in the north arm of Great Slave Lake out of Trout Rock Lodge in the Northwest Territories. Hanks—a pike guru—wrote *Fly Fishing in the Northwest Territories of Canada* (1996). So far, the finny denizens in the north arm had straightened swivel snaps and wrecked wire leader cable splice connectors, bending my 8-weight fly rod nearly full circle.

"Try bringing the pike to reel as soon as possible so you get the line out of the way," Hanks shouted as I hooked another King Kong–sized pike. "Otherwise you'll get finger burns. You'll also have better line control."

It was crash course in landing big pike—with daily catch rates in the dozens, I was on a steep learning curve! I've subsequently fly fished for pike on many lakes in Canada's North Country and have refined my fly fishing approach to these challenging fish.

Unlike the follow-up after hook sets on trout (where it's advisable to first bring the fish under control by handling the fly line before trying to bring it to reel), in the case of large pike, it's best to capitalize on the breaking power of your reel when landing pike. A large-arbour reel is a definite asset when trying to control these ferocious fish that strike aggressively and with a vengeance, because you can bring in that much more line quickly. Let the drag, the flex in the fly rod and the stretch in the fly line tire large pike before trying to land them.

Hanks recommends medium-action fly rods for pike as opposed to fast-action rods because tossing large pike flies is a lot like throwing a wet baseball. Don't go below an 8-weight fly rod—a 9- or 10-weight rod won't be overdoing it for large pike.

Use a sink tip line during spring (before aquatic plants are abundant), then switch to a floating line in summer. I recommend a minimum of 100 yards of backing, although large pike usually don't run far.

When fly fishing for pike, tungsten or braided leaders are essential; otherwise the fish's sharp teeth will cut the monofilament tippet or leader. Ideally, you'll need 18- to 20-pound (minimum) tungsten or steel leader capped with 2 feet of 40-pound monofilament shock leader on a floating or sink tip fly line. However, a stainless steel TyGer 15-pound leader is a good bet, and even conventional steel or braided leaders used traditionally on monofilament lines. Short leaders will turn the fly line over better than long leaders with a sink tip line,

but you can use a longer leader with a floating line to get your flies down into the strike zone.

Also, practice tying clinch or slip knots with wire leaders because the cable splice connectors that are supplied by the manufacturer with shock tippets will fail eventually. Further, there never seem to be enough of them in the packages supplied by the manufacturers. These knots will hold well when tied directly onto a large pike fly. You'll need wire cutters to trim the shock tippet cable to ease casting. Use stainless steel ball bearing swivels with clasps to secure tippets to fly line that can't be pulled straight when fly fishing for pike—you can use clasps to fasten large flies to wire leaders and they'll still cast well. Pike have a burst speed of about 20 miles per hour, so when they strike, instant pressure is applied to all components of your fishing outfit, and any weak spots will fail: swivel snaps and bearings, cable splice connectors, knots, possibly rod tips or even reels.

Fly fishing for pike is challenging because they're so hard on tackle.

Fly fishing guru Chris Hanks prefers black and chartreuse streamers for pike.

Pike flies fall into four basic patterns: bunnies, divers, streamers and poppers, typically with gaudy colors—chartreuse, bright red and yellow; however, black and white flies are also good producers. Pike flies recommended in *Lefty Kreh's Ultimate Guide to Fly Fishing* (2003) include Lefty's Deceivers in red and white, chartreuse and white and olive and red, Clouser Minnow (same colours) and Black Rabbit Leech.

Try targeteing northern pike in shallow bays beside emergent vegetation.

I used four hand-tied patterns on 2–6X long streamer hooks for my trip on Great Slave Lake: three colour patterns (yellow, white and black) of rabbit strip, clousers and an orange cone head streamer from my box, as well as a chartreuse clouser with a chain (used as weight) from Hanks' fly box. All caught pike. When it comes to dressings, synthetic material sheds water better than natural dressing, which can get quite soggy and hard to cast. There are no definitive must-have pike flies; of many patterns on the market, most will likely catch pike.

Don't leave home without your hook sharpener. Many large pike hooks are made of stainless steel and don't always have a razor sharp edge when they come from the manufacturer.

Fly fishing for pike from a boat is quite straightforward. Start by searching out pike habitat in shallow bays, structures along the shoreline, the edges of emergent aquatic vegetation and shallow channels between islands and the shore. Target pike in fairly shallow water in spring. Pike will move offshore into deeper water during summer as lake temperatures rise, and then move back into the shallows in autumn when the water cools.

Use a straight-line cast to present a pike fly, then strip your line during the retrieve. Vary the strip to entice strikes, and pay attention during the final stages because pike often stalk a fly and attack it at the last moment. Also, it's quite common for a strike immediately after the fly touches the water, or shortly afterwards—watch for the wake of attacking fish in the latter situation.

If there's a breeze, it doesn't hurt to troll (using the wind drift) in shallow bays, which can be a productive technique. Also, trolling has its place in narrows between islands and the shore where there's a bit of depth—particularly during the early morning and evening, when pike seem to hunt most actively.

To save your casting arm, it's best to leave the line in the water to load your rod when fishing with 8- to 10-weight rods. Lift it at a 90 degree angle, pause on your back cast and then cast forward; lean into your cast by putting your shoulder into the cast to punch the fly line towards your target.

Action on pike is affected by water temperature; pike prefer a temperature in the range of 18–20° C. You can expect hookups to drop off if a low pressure system moves in and lowers water temperatures in prime pike habitat.

I'm sold on fish cradles over landing nets for handling large pike. Cradles are easy on the fish and don't cause any damage, which is always a possibility with landing nets. The pike stays in the water and remains relatively docile while in a cradle—it gets

oxygen from the water and recovers from its struggle, ready to swim freely in short order.

Wear protective gloves when handling pike, which are hard to grip because of their blocky shape and slippery body. Wet the protective glove before handling pike to minimize possible damage to their protective coating of slime. Use long needlenose pliers to dislodge the fly. Sometimes it's necessary to use jaw spreaders (also called fish gags) to keep their big mouths open when removing a hook. Use jaw spreaders equipped with rubber ends so they won't harm a pike's soft mouth. If a pike is winded, cradle it in your hands (submerged) for a while until it recovers and swims off on its own—rock it back and forth in the water to pass oxygenated water over its gills if it appears weak.

If you follow the above tips, you'll catch lots of pike and land some fine trophies.

Use a fish cradle to land a large pike.

Chapter 5

North of 60 Insect Hatches

What a tourist terms a plague of insects, the fly fisher calls a great hatch.
—Patrick F. McManus

There is a dearth of published information regarding insect hatches in Canada's north. For this reason, I am including information about early, mid and late season hatches as an aid to itinerant fly fishers to better prepare them for gearing up their fly box.

Insect studies north of 60 are still very much a work in progress, regarding hatches. There have been insect collections throughout representative areas, but not on many waters. Yukon has been sampled

the best. In some parts of the Northwest Territories and Nunavut, collections have been spotty. The collection dates of many species of adult caddis flies, mayflies and stoneflies have been documented, however, so they can be classified according to early, mid or late season hatches.

The scientific literature I've reviewed has documentation of the following (approximate) number of species belonging to the key insect orders of most interest to fly fishers: 30 species of mayfly, 70 stoneflies,

Mid season insect hatches North of 60 are dominated by chironomids, caddis flies and stoneflies.

There is not a lot of information regarding insect hatches specific to Nunavut.

75 black flies, 100 chironomids and 145 caddis flies. There have also been over 30 species of dragonfly documented, which hatch by mid-June, although these are not as commonly fly fished. Entomologists consider these numbers as being minimum estimates and lament the lack of northern studies to date.

The life histories of many common insects from the north are known in southern Canada and elsewhere. Consequently, it's possible to connect the dots, so to speak, for the north in terms of emergence patterns. Actually, it's even easier—the collection dates of adult insects are often given in the literature, confirming anticipated hatches. Anglers should expect the distribution of northern insect hatches to be more restricted in duration, and the initial time of emergence to be several months later, compared with more southern locales. Research has shown that the sequence of emergence—which is likely temperature dependent—of various species of aquatic insects is strikingly similar when the southern versus northern distribution is compared. One final note: northern early and mid season insect hatches appear to be abbreviated, and the late season hatches appear to start and end sooner than in the south.

One of the most important sources of information regarding aquatic insects is a book published by the Canadian Museum of Nature, Ottawa, entitled *Insects of the Yukon* (1997) and co-edited by H.V. Danks and J.A. Downes. It contains chapters on the key insect orders of interest to the serious fly fisher: Dipterans (flies), Emphemeroptera (mayflies), Plecoptera (stoneflies) and Trichopetera (caddis flies).

Mayflies: An Angler's Study of Trout Water Ephemeroptera (1997), by Malcolm Knopp and Robert Cormier, provides good insight into the biology and life histories of mayflies. I particularly like the hatch charts,

There are practically no bugs in the Ekaluk River on Victoria Island, Nunavut.

which illustrate the major emergence patterns in an easy-to-understand format, and although it doesn't cover the area north of 60, it's a good text nonetheless and provides a good review of the ecology of mayflies.

Information regarding key insect hatches in various rivers and lakes is the bread and butter of various fishing lodges and is one of the reasons that many people hire a guide when fishing in the north. Certain lodge owners have good reasons for not making this information public knowledge and hope fly fishers understand that they would rather not disclose their trade secrets. Having said that, certain lodges and fishing guides have shared their knowledge with me, and based on additional information in the scientific literature, it's possible to provide a report on the key hatches. In particular, Hans van Klinken, from Holland, kindly supplied me with hatch charts based on his fly fishing experience in Yukon. I'd also like to acknowledge Wayne Witherspoon of Frontier Fishing Lodge on

Great Slave Lake, who provided me with information about hatches in that part of the Canadian north.

As a general rule, the serious fly fisher should be prepared for all manner of insect hatches from ice-out until late autumn.

Hans van Klinken recommends the following damselfly nymph patterns: Whitlock's Damsel, Barr's Damsel Nymph and A.K. Swimming Damsel. His recommended adult patterns are Burk's Adult Damsel and Barr's Damsel.

He recommends the following dragonfly nymph patterns: Kaufmann's Lake Dragon, Whitlock's Dragon and Gierach's Dragon. His recommended scud patterns are Epoxy Back Scud, Braggy Shrimp, Kaufmann's Scud and Bead Heads.

Early Season

Some northerners claim that spring is rather fleeting north of 60, saying that one day there's snow on the ground, and the next thing you know, it's summer. Consequently, in Yukon, Northwest Territories and Nunavut, early season hatches are abbreviated by southern standards. Generally speaking, ice-out is from April to mid-May on rivers, and from late May to early June on lakes. But not always—Tincup Lake in Yukon was still frozen over in late June a few years ago. Reports on traditional knowledge indicate that the spring breakup is now occurring earlier than it did historically, as well as the freeze-up being later, likely due to climate change and global warming.

The north is called the Land of the Midnight Sun for good reason—during late spring and early summer there are virtually 24 hours of daylight. Although early season hatches may be abbreviated or in some cases extended, relatively speaking, the early season hatches might run the gamut from early April to mid-July, depending on the location in this vast region. For instance, the early season hatch happens in April on south Mackenzie Basin rivers but not until mid-July on Great Bear Lake, the east arm of Great Slave Lake and in the Barren Grounds, all of which are situated at a more northerly latitude.

Rivers

Several species of snow fly (*Nemoura*) are present in Yukon and will emerge as soon as there is open water. Snow flies are also present in flowing waters in the Northwest Territories. These small, dark stoneflies can often be found crawling on the snow and ice along the water's edge; fish feed on them on top of the water on warm, sunny spring days. Snow flies are dark brown, reddish brown or black in colour and are common even in March in more southern

Early sesaon hatches in Yukon are dominated by stoneflies and caddis flies.

Stonefly hatches can be highly synchronized or spotty on northern rivers.

locations. Use Pheasant Tail Nymph size 12–16 flies as an imitation. Snow flies' emergence is staggered during the early season, and given species may have long emergence periods up to two months.

Stoneflies live for extended periods as adults (one to several weeks). Their hatches can be highly synchronized and in phenomenal numbers or spotty with low numbers. While a great many species of stonefly live in Canada's north, the few species of Skwala and salmon flies (Perlidae and Pteronarcydae) present are of the most interest to fly fishers—these are giants among stoneflies. I've seen Skwala hatches of biblical proportions on the Peace River in northern Alberta in late May/early June, which likely occur on some of the large rivers farther north at about the same time. These hatches are

brief, occurring shortly after ice-out, when millions of stonefly nymphs crawl out of the water during the course of an evening and subsequently molt into adults overnight before beginning their mating rituals. Salmon flies are less common. Stimulators (golden, olive, orange or royal) and Egg Laying *Pteronaracys* sizes 10–14 are good patterns during this time.

Tiny mayfly species (*Baetis*) are early emergers, some of which have two hatches annually—the first shortly after ice breakup and a second late season hatch. Use Blue Winged Olives sizes 16–22 when adults are on the water or in the air. Mayflies belong to the order Ephemeroptera—ephemeral, meaning temporary in existence. These insects have a long aquatic stage, often taking a year to develop as nymphs before they emerge from the water and metamorphose into adults, after which they live for only about 24 hours. Adult mayflies have no mouthparts; consequently, they can't eat and their sole purpose is to mate and lay eggs to re-populate the species before dying. They're not strong flyers and tend to be most obvious in the evening when the winds are calm, at which time they swarm to find mates. Hexagena mayflies (fly fisher terminology for large mayflies) are also present and generally dwell in the soft bottoms of northern lakes and backwaters of rivers and streams. They start to emerge during the early season.

The dreaded black fly—a small, biting Dipteran or fly—is one of the most common insects that typify early season hatches throughout all of the north. Adults are considered more of a nuisance than mosquitoes. Black flies are filter feeders in their larval stage, and they anchor themselves on rocks, sucking in passing food particles suspended in the water. They're generally most troublesome near the mouths of rivers, where they can literally carpet the substrate. There are 40-plus different black fly species, which fall into both early and late season species in the north. The Black Gnat wet, sizes 10–14, and Black Gnat dry, sizes 12–20, are the most common patterns, as well as size 16–20 Griffith's Gnats.

Net-spinning and free-living caddis flies—commonly called sedges or sandflies—are fairly common throughout much of the north but typically are not characterized by an abundance of early season hatches in northern rivers. If you see fish rising but no adult sedges in the air, try a size 12–16 Klinkhammer Special (emerger), originally tied as an emerging caddis fly, which comes in various colours (black, brown, cream, claret, orange, olive, etc.).

Black flies typify early season hatches throughout the north, including on the Tree River, Nunavut.

Lakes

If there is one insect that's universal during the early season hatch, it is the ubiquitous midge, better known to anglers as chironomids, or bloodworms in their larval stage. In their aquatic form, bloodworms dwell in the sediment of lakes. They're often bright red in colour, full of hemoglobin to capture what little dissolved oxygen is present in the often stagnant water in the mud/bottom water interface in which they dwell throughout their aquatic larval stage. Brassies, Chironomid Larva Nymphs and Chironomid Reds are good larval imitations, while Chironomid Pupa and bead head Pupa patterns cover pupal stages. As adults, they're often confused with mosquitoes but are actually harmless little flies, primarily distinguishable by their feathery antennae. Numerous dry fly patterns imitate adult or emerging chironomids: Chan's Chironomid, TDC, Rising Midge Pupa, Griffith's Gnat, Humpy, CDC Hatching Midge, CDC Midge Adult or Mosquito, to name but a few patterns. Use size 16–22 hooks. Look for adults near shore and emerging pupa at the interface of the surface water and air. When present, a good option is to fish a pupa pattern on a long (9-foot) leader set a foot or so off the lake bottom, using a strike indicator—just watch the action!

Another form of chironomid, the chaoborus fly, a non-biting midge called phantom midges or glass worms in their larval stage, is also an early emerging insect. Adults live for less than a week, and these midges emerge again in mid to late season. In its larval form it's practically transparent, hence the name phantom midge—it's distinguishable by black, paired hydrostatic air sacs anteriorly and posteriorly that are used for buoyancy. As larvae, phantom midges spend their days just off the lake bottom. Some instars are noted for daily diurnal vertical migrations from bottom to top and back again. This is why larval imitations are fished: to capitalize on its presence in the upper water column during the late evening. Use the Phantom Midge size 10–14 fly pattern to imitate these larvae. Adult phantom midges resemble mosquitoes, being about the same size, without a long proboscis and having hairy wings, feathery antennae and being pale in colour. Adults emerge simultaneously, swarm, mate, live for a few days and then die.

A red bead head Chironomid (bloodworm) is a good choice for lakes during the early season.

An Elk Hair Caddis is a good all-around pattern during all seasons North of 60.

Various species of *Brachycentrus*, case-building caddis flies (or sedges), are early emergers—I've watched both lake trout at Dezadeash Lake, Yukon, and northern pike on Great Slave Lake, NWT, slurp adults off the surface in early June—the size of the trout and pike that were feeding on these sedges surprised me, being in the range of 15 to 25 pounds. Popular fly patterns are caddis larvae/pupae in olive, tan and cream, the Elk Hair Caddis and Goddard Caddis, all in sizes 12–16. On Wellesley Lake, also in Yukon, legendary hatches of large sedges attract lake trout in spring, particularly off the immense reef on the north shore. However, if the weather is cold and breakup is later than normal, the hatch could occur in mid season. If you see fish rising but no sedges are in the air, another good choice is the Klinkhammer Special (emerger). I've fished for Arctic grayling on Tincup Lake, Yukon, with Hans van Klinken, who invented this fly and can attest to its effectiveness. Plop the Klinkhammer Special in the vicinity of rising Arctic grayling and watch them slurp it from the surface. This fly is a keeper, right up there with the Elk Hair Caddis as a good all-around pattern. Hans also recommends Tom Thumb, Humpy, Stimulators and Emergent Sparkle Pupa patterns.

Baetis mayfly species are early emergers on lakes as well as rivers. Use the same flies, Blue Winged Olives sizes 16–22, when adults are on the water. Other mayfly patterns recommended by Hans van Klinken are the Parachute Adams, CDC Biot Comparadun, Cahill and Realistica.

During spring, try the following streamers for lake trout: Matuka Sculpins (olive or brown) sizes 4–10; brown, black or olive Marabou Leeches sizes 2–8; various Muddlers and the cone head Bunny Worm, sizes 2–6; brown, black, olive or purple Woolly Buggers, and the Egg Sucking Leech sizes 2–8. These patterns imitate bait fish and leeches, which are lake trout prey.

Mid Season

Mid season hatches encompass the period from mid-July to the end of August. The average temperature in Whitehorse, Yukon, is 14° C in July and 12.3° C in August; days are still long, with an average of 19 and 17 hours of daylight during July and August, respectively, in Yukon. Typically, the first frost occurs on August 30 in Yukon. Although cold fronts do move through and it's possible to experience the odd snowstorm during the mid season, for the most part days are warm, sunny and downright invigorating, what with all the daylight.

Pesky no-see-ums, horseflies, black flies and even mosquitoes are still present in the north during the period of the mid season insect hatches, so don't leave home without some insect repellent, even though black flies seem to be immune to most repellents.

Fly Fishing in the Northwest Territories of Canada (1996), by Chris Hanks, is a must-read for any fly fishers interested in fly fishing the north. Hanks has a chapter about fly fishing for lake trout and Arctic grayling in mid-July on Great Bear Lake, where I obtained a different insight regarding his recommended patterns compared to my own experiences in Yukon.

Larry Nagy, former co-owner of Tincup Wilderness Lodge on Tincup Lake and Tincup Creek, says that most of the major hatches are over and done with by early July. Based on my experience, however, there's an almost daily hatch of midges on most lakes and the occasional hatch of pale morning duns on most waters in the evening, occasionally two or more, but very little surface activity during the day, during the mid season.

Try caddis patterns for the mid season North of 60 if all else fails.

A Royal Wulff is a go-to pattern for Arctic grayling.

Rivers

Various species of tiny mayflies (*Baetis*) are present in swift-flowing streams throughout much of the north. Some of these species have two or more generations per year; consequently it's not unusual to find adults in early, mid or late season hatches. According to the scientific literature, the pale morning dun (PMD) probably occurs in Yukon and is known to be present in the Northwest Territories, typically as a mid season emerger. Use a size 14–18 hook for PMD patterns. The western green drake is also present in Yukon, and also known for mid season hatches. Use a size 10–14 hook for adult green drakes. Hexagena mayflies (large mayflies) generally dwell in the soft bottoms of northern lakes and backwaters of rivers and streams and start to emerge during the mid season in the Northwest Territories.

Both yellow and lime sally stonefly species (i.e., sallies) are present in Yukon and Northwest Territories. These mid season emergers are relatively small stoneflies, compared with the much larger Skwala

and salmon flies. Adult sallies are active from mid-June through mid-August. Females will swarm over the water and lay eggs in riffles and runs, providing excellent dry fly fishing opportunities. A good choice for yellow or lime sally stoneflies is a yellow or lime trude on a size 14–16 Mustad hook. Trudes are attractor patterns that imitate nothing in particular but float well in rough water and are visible. Snow flies are also present in the Northwest Territories, as well as several types of sallies having been reported even in the Horton River, one of the most remote and northern rivers in the Northwest Territories.

The venerable October caddis is present in Yukon; it belongs to the genus *Dicosmoecus*, of which two species are present. In the southern Rockies, they are seen most often in late season hatches, typically September to October, but in Yukon, adults have been collected during the mid season (not the late season) hatch. These are big, lumbering sedges that are clumsy fliers and seem to have a hard time remaining airborne; females hit the water

A black Woolly Bugger is an old standby pattern in both still waters and rivers.

like they're about to crash land before fluttering off again. I spotted a solitary October caddis on Tincup Creek late in the afternoon during a mid-August trip, which is customary of their behaviour down south (i.e., flying solo). They are the giants of the caddis world, dark sedges with large orange bodies. Dry fly patterns include an orange or cream stimulator and an Elk Hair Caddis tied with a pale orange or pale yellow body, hook size 10. On dry flies and lake trout, Hanks found that size 12–16 Nelson's Caddis flies took 3- to 6-pound trout on the Kazan River in Nunavut.

There are relatively few species of chironomids in flowing water in the north.

There are mid season hatches of black fly species in the north, bearing in mind that in the Northwest Territories and Nunavut, this would be early August. The Black Gnat wet in sizes 10–14 and Black Gnat dry, sizes 12–20, are the most common patterns, as well as size 16–20 Griffith's Gnats.

Lakes

The chaoborus fly (a non-biting midge), called phantom midges or glass worms by fly fishers, is a mid season emerging insect—adults live for less than a week. (Note that these midges emerge in early and late season also.) Use the Phantom Midge size 10–14 fly pattern to imitate midge larvae.

Hanks used Goddard Caddis sizes 10–14 in olive and mottled-grey and brown on Great Bear Lake in the Northwest Territories to catch lake trout on dry flies. He didn't trim them when he wanted a fluttering caddis, but rather nipped a few hairs to create flapping wings. For the sedentary sedges, he trimmed the body into the tight triangular tent characteristic of a resting caddis adult.

Brian Dack, who operates Kluane Wilderness Lodge on Wellesley Lake, reported build-ups of travelling sedge hatches in early July, making for great dry fly fishing

A bead head Ice Cream Cone Chironomid resembles a phanton midge, good for lake whitefish.

for lake trout and lake whitefish, right in front of the lodge. Sedges may hatch in mid season if ice breakup is delayed.

There are relatively few mayfly hatches on lakes during the mid season, excepting sporadic PMD hatches.

Lake whitefish are common in most lakes and are also present in many rivers. They can be taken on a fly. The key insect hatches for this species are normally late July or early August in the Northwest Territories, earlier in Yukon. Use Blue Winged Olives size 16–18 when adult mayflies are hatching. In the case of caddis flies/ larvae, try Caddis larvae/pupae in olive, tan or cream sizes 12–16, Elk Hair Caddis sizes 12–16 and Goddard Caddis sizes 12–16. For a nymph, the Gold Ribbed Hare's Ear, size 16, is a good choice.

Late Season

Autumn comes early in the northern territories, and by mid-August, the autumn colours begin to show as temperatures dip to near freezing overnight. This is a period of transition and can be quite windy, with unsettled weather and cold fronts moving through. Snowstorms are probable during the period of late season hatches in the north. Hatches are almost over for the year and insect activity can be sporadic; it's catch as catch can for the itinerant fly fisher. However, there are some old standby patterns that will catch northern fish during the late season, which extends from early September to mid-October.

Rivers

Many species of black flies are late emergers in the north. The Black Gnat wet sizes 10–14 and Black Gnat dry sizes 12–20 are the most common patterns, as well as size 16–20 Griffith's Gnats.

Baetis mayflies are known from Yukon, Northwest Territories and Nunavut and occasionally hatch in the late season, though they are more commonly seen in early and mid season. Use Blue Winged

There's a paucity of late season hatches in the high Arctic.

Olives sizes 16–22 when adults are on the water or in the air.

Some species of lime sallies hatch during the late season.

Lakes

The chaoborus fly (a non-biting midge), called phantom midge or glass worm by fly fishers, emerges in the late season as well as early and mid seasons—adults live for less than a week. Use the Phantom Midge sizes 10–14 fly pattern to imitate midge larvae.

A Chernobyl Ant is good during the late season.

Don't overlook terrestrial insect fly patterns, which are common in the north. For example, there are 17 species of grasshoppers in Yukon alone and all manner of other terrestrial insects: hundreds of species of true bugs, leaf hoppers, ants, butterflies, moths and beetles to name but a few. Key attractor patterns such as the Chernobyl Ant, Turk's Tarantula and Madame X work well, along with various hopper patterns (e.g., MoJoe Hopper and Parachute Frankenhopper patterns)—I'd use size 8–10 attractor flies.

Anything is possible in the world of fly fishing. A Yukon fishing guide related a story to me about some red-hot action on lake trout when a horde of yellow jackets floated down an inlet stream to Kathleen Lake, which drove the trout nuts while it lasted. The guide had no idea where all the wasps came from—possibly their nest fell in the water—but it didn't matter to the trout!

Chapter 6

Etiquette and Ethics of Fly Fishing

Creeps and idiots cannot conceal themselves for long on a fishing trip.

–John Gierach

Angling Etiquette

Etiquette is defined as the conventional rules for conduct or behaviour in polite society. In angling parlance, however, they're not written down as such and (perhaps) that's part of the problem with regard to what I see as an alarming lack of angling etiquette. Furthermore, these "rules" tend to change from one location to another, depending on the nature of the fishery and even the size of a stream.

What may be good etiquette in one part of British Columbia may not be acceptable elsewhere in that province. For example, around Fernie, BC, a fly fishing Mecca, it's fair game for an angler to stake out a pool or run on local streams and fish there until he or she feels it's time to move on. But on steelhead streams near Terrace, British Columbia, it's expected that anglers will fish through a pool and then move on to the next one; it would be poor etiquette to try to stake out a pool when fishing for steelhead.

On small streams, it's best for a couple of anglers to rotate fishing at pools.

> *Somebody just back of you while you are fishing is as bad as someone looking over your shoulder while you write a letter to your girl.*
>
> –Ernest Hemingway

One reason I'd like to address conventional fishing etiquette is that I've had some bad experiences with some fishermen and fishing guides who have displayed poor fishing etiquette and soured my trips. Perhaps my rant will change some anglers' behaviour for the better and make for a more pleasant outing when on the water.

Once, a fishing guide dropped a party of four clients right on top of me and my partners while we were walk-and-wade fishing on a foothills stream in southwestern Alberta. The guided party split up and moved upstream and downstream of my party, effectively cutting us out of any options—we really had nowhere to go. Proper etiquette dictated that the guide

should have taken his party to another part of the stream, so as not to interfere with our trip. It was an uncomfortable experience for all of us and could have been avoided.

On another occasion, a couple of non-resident anglers came up from downstream and fished through a pool that my son and I were already fishing, moving right on to the next pool. I was flabbergasted! In this case, proper etiquette dictates that this party should have walked on past us until they were out of sight and then resumed fishing.

Many fishing guides stagger start times to minimize conflicts with other drift boats on popular rivers in Alberta and British Columbia. Most guides head out at about 9:00 AM; consequently, an early start at 8:00 AM, or a bit later, at 10:00 AM, will likely see less traffic. Anglers can do likewise when deciding on start times for their own fishing trips. During floats, guides also try to move over to the other side of the river when they encounter drift boats, or pull over until the boats are out of sight. It's proper etiquette for anglers in a drift boat to remove their lines from the water when fishing past shore anglers until they've drifted downstream so as not spoil

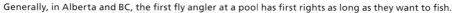

Generally, in Alberta and BC, the first fly angler at a pool has first rights as long as they want to fish.

the fun for those on shore—they were there first, and as such have first rights.

When fly fishing from a drift boat (or raft), the person up front generally has the best shot at rising fish, or even when blind casting, while the sport in the rear picks up the leavings and tries to clean the table. You may want to alternate during a float so both anglers have a more level playing field. Personally, I like the aft station, so it doesn't bother me if other people like to be up front. In any event, talk about rotating positions with your partner before you start so as not to create any hard feelings. It's incumbent on the sports in both the bow and stern stations in a drift boat to be fully cognizant of the guide in the middle at all times for safety reasons, and cast accordingly. Also, the person up front can't see where his partner is casting, so it falls upon the person in the rear to hold off on his cast until the angler up front has completed casting to avoid tangles.

In a canoe or jet boat, the guide will be in the aft station near the motor, and he or she should keep a low profile and not bob around to make casting easier for the sports.

On small streams, if you're fishing with a buddy it's a good idea to lay out the ground rules before you start fishing. One way to be fair is to let the first up catch one fish in a pool or run and then let the partner have a go at it. In some circles, if the angler who is first up even misses a good rise, he's expected to step aside and wait out a turn because it's quite likely that the very act of missing a strike could put that particular fish down.

While conventional rules (except for steelhead fishing) dictate that whoever is first in a pool has first rights, I've always felt that you shouldn't hog a pool just because you happened to stake it out first. Fish it for a while and then move on to let

somebody else have a try if other anglers are in the area. Always ask the locals what goes for proper angling etiquette in their area because they're in the best position to understand regional nuances. Regarding steelhead, it's not considered fair practice to stake out a pool and stay there just because you were first in line.

Fishing for Atlantic salmon in New Brunswick may well be the ultimate experience in Canadian angling etiquette because of exclusive rights granted to private individuals for salmon fishing on certain rivers, and/or riparian rights on stretches of rivers (that in some cases pre-date Confederation of Canada), which are or could be sublet to guides and outfitters. During an Atlantic salmon fishing trip at Pond's Resort on the Miramichi River in New Brunswick, guide Donald Beek explained the local customs and traditions associated with these laws. Non-residents must be accompanied by

Proper etiquette calls for moving through steelhead pools.

a guide; they rotate through select pools (on one side of the river only in some cases because the rights may apply to only half of the riverbed) on particular assigned parts of a river, and at certain times of the day. You basically have the pool and river to yourself for a certain period of time and are expected to share in the fishing experience with other guided clients, so as not to monopolize choice spots. An angler starts fishing at the head of the pool, then works his way downstream towards the tail end; he makes two or three down and out casts, subsequently takes two or three steps down river, and so on until he reaches the end of the pool; he would then repeat this rotation. Unless both banks of the river are sublet, it's considered poor etiquette to cast beyond the midpoint of the stream. Everybody shares in the chance of hooking the "King's fish," which can be hard to catch under even the best of circumstances; consequently, there's an incentive for private owners to better conserve the salmon. We got lucky, landing several grilse and adult Atlantic salmon up to about 17 pounds.

Catch-and-release Fishing Ethics

Back in the 1990s, catch and release became more and more common in Canada and to a lesser degree in the United States as a fisheries management tool to sustain fish populations. Also, some species were being brought under this regime strictly for fisheries conservation purposes. In some situations, zero bag limits came into effect where fish stocks were too low to sustain a harvest. In other cases, zero limits were intended to provide a unique fishing experience, such as on heritage rivers. In yet other situations, minimum size limits were instituted to ensure natural reproduction.

Various regulation scenarios require that certain species of fish, or fish of a certain size, be returned to the water unharmed. Some anglers practice catch-and-release fishing by choice, even though keeping their catch may be perfectly legal. However, fishing regulations are designed to sustain fish populations by natural

Keep a fish in the water as much as possible when it's going to be caught and released.

Don't squeeze a fish around the tail or body, or you'll damage organs or the outer layer of cells.

reproduction, and it is perfectly acceptable to take some fish from many water bodies home to eat, from a population perspective. Fish are a nutritious source of protein and are tasty.

This brings me to the matter of ethics pertaining to catch and release, particularly the humane treatment, care and handling of fish. Regulations such as minimum size limits and zero bag limits have been in effect for a long time, at least since the 1930s in Alberta. Care and handling of fish have been of concern for at least this long. It is important that anglers treat fish with the care and respect they deserve, but if they don't, it is often out of ignorance of fish biology and fish behaviour.

Fish are cold-blooded animals that take on the temperature of the water in which they live. This does not mean they do not have any feelings or sensory perceptions. To the contrary, fish are sensitive to odours, touch, vibrations and underwater movements. Sight is not as acute as the other senses even in clear water, but fish can see in every direction, in colour, and have binocular vision. They also have depth perception, although this is restricted to a small zone

in front of their snout. If they have a failing (from an anthropomorphism perspective), it is that they lack eyelids and can't blink like some cuddly, warm-blooded mammal; consequently, they don't seem to evoke the same emotions in people as the likes of kittens, seal pups, fawns, etc.

After a fish is hooked, both its respiration and heart rate increase during capture, handling and also when it is out of water, which are classic signs of physiological stress. Research also indicates that fish can feel pain, although there is still some dispute about this. We don't know if fish experience pain the way humans do. Although fish have tough scales on their body surface, these scales are actually covered by a layer of living cells. It is this layer of cells that is responsible for secreting mucous on the surface of fish, as well as for the growth of scales. This layer of living cells can be damaged relatively easily if fish are handled improperly. Such damage may lead to infections, and sometimes even death. It is not uncommon for fish to develop severe fungal infections when this surface layer of scales is damaged. Properly handled, however, fish can be caught and released many times with minimal impact.

About the only noticeable damage to fish that have been caught and released several times may be to the mandibles on the edge of the jaw, as these can tear, occasionally coming right off, unfortunately. It is important that fish be treated humanely and handled carefully, to minimize angling mortality and to sustain their populations.

There has always been a lot of debate about proper handling techniques, which I find quite humorous. You see, things haven't changed a whole lot over the years in terms of do's and don'ts when it comes to catching and releasing fish. I read some fishing regulations for Alberta dated 1930, and they said it all, just as well, way back then as now. To quote the regulations of the day, "When an undersized fish is hooked, the angler shall draw it to him without removing it from the water to any greater extent than is necessary. Before grasping it to remove the hook, he shall wet his hand or, preferably, have on his hand a wet cotton or woollen glove. The fish shall be kept in the water while the hook is being removed, and held as lightly as possible, so as to avoid injury by pressure. When the hook is in the lip it shall be removed by turning the shank towards the hook, and when it is swallowed so as to need the use of a disgorger, such shall be placed under the hook and moved along it so as push the hook out, the line being held taut enough to prevent the disgorger slipping off the hook." While this is hardly what I would call "plain English," it is the way things should be done.

Nowadays, many people are motivated to fish for different reasons than they were in days gone by, when people fished primarily for food. Today's anglers are more likely to release fish than ever before. Furthermore, the more experienced anglers release more of their catch than other, less-experienced fishermen. Relatively few anglers release fish just because it is required by law. You can improve your future fishing if you carefully release all fish under the legal length, and those you do not intend to eat. Fish that are quickly and carefully returned to the water will survive, giving you a chance to catch them

Handle a fish as little as possible when removing it from the water to take a picture.

again. Take the following steps to improve their survival chances.

Don't play a fish to exhaustion. The goal is for it to swim away on its own after it has been landed. If it appears tired, cup it in your hands until it is rested and able to swim off on its own. The time involved in this step may vary from a few seconds to several minutes. Hold the fish into the current or waves so that water flows over its gills to speed its recovery. Exhaustive exercise, such as that associated with angling, may lead to "delayed mortality" of fish, which is thought to be a result of a physiological disturbance within the white muscle of fish.

Twist the hook from its mouth if at all possible. This is not hard to do with a little experience. Scientific findings indicate that use of barbed or barbless flies plays virtually no role in subsequent mortality of trout caught by anglers. There is no biological basis for barbed hook restrictions in artificial flies and lure fisheries for trout. Anglers who support the use of barbless hooks should do so voluntarily. However, do not tear out the hook. Work it gently back and forth until it is free. Never pull a hook from a fish's throat or stomach. It is much better just to cut the line—many hooks will rust away.

Keep a fish in water as much as possible if you intend to release it. Keeping the fish in fresh, oxygenated water will minimize stress. If you must remove a fish from the water, handle it as little as possible. Do not put your fingers in the gill covers; don't hold the fish by its eye sockets. Hold a fish firmly and upside down to reduce its struggles. A fish dropped on the ground or in a boat has a poor chance of survival.

It is very important not to damage the surface layer of living cells that covers the scales. For larger species such as northern

Carefully release any fish you don't intend to eat.

pike and lake trout, use a wetted cotton or woollen glove. I don't think that a wetted rubber glove (surgical type) would be much different than a cotton or wool glove, provided you handle the fish with care. A cotton glove will help give you a better grip than a bare hand. Don't squeeze a fish by the tail or around its body, or you will damage the outer layer of cells or internal organs. This is especially true for small fish, particularly trout. Fish that have been handled roughly can develop a "brand" or imprint of a person's hand where too much pressure was applied while holding onto them.

If you practice these recommendations there will be minimal angling mortality. You will also be treating fish with the care and respect they so rightly deserve. And to top it all off, you will be a good sportsman who will bring credit to the sport of angling.

The finest gift you can give to any fisherman is to put a good fish back, and who knows if the fish that you caught isn't someone else's gift to you?

–Lee Wulff

Chapter 7

Canadian Fly Fishing Hot Spots

There will be days when the fishing is better than one's most optimistic forecast, others when it is far worse. Either is a gain over just staying home.

–Roderick Haig-Brown

Canada is blessed with many outstanding locations to go fly fishing for a variety of top species: Atlantic salmon, Arctic char, lake trout and steelhead being at the top of the list. There are, however, many other fine species, such as Arctic grayling, cutthroat trout, brown trout, bull trout, coho salmon, northern pike, rainbow trout, etc., which while not necessarily as large as the most famed species, are nonetheless highly prized game fish.

The Elk River: BC's Cutthroat Trout Mecca

The Elk River is unquestionably one of Canada's top streams for west slope cutthroat trout, long renowned as a go-to stream for dry fly fishing enthusiasts in particular.

I've enjoyed some fine fishing on the Elk River in British Columbia's Kootenays, a large freestone river that arguably rates

The Elk River is a top stream for cutthroat trout fishing.

An Elk River cutthroat trout.

as one of Canada's best streams for cutthroat trout. Mind you, some Elk River tributaries match the mother lode parent stream in terms of both size and abundance of cutthroat trout because of the fish's migratory nature in the Elk River drainage; no trip to this region should focus entirely on the Elk River. In fact, I'd encourage anglers to do some exploring on their own and seek out trout in the many tributaries to the Elk River. You will be pleasantly surprised at just how good fishing can be in the Fording River, Michel Creek and the Wigwam, to name but a few, and *their* tributaries. It's possible to catch cutthroats ranging 12–18 inches long, with some crowding 20 inches or more, throughout the Elk River watershed.

I've fished the Elk River during July, August and September, throughout all the key sections from points upstream of Elkford down to above Elko, a distance of river about 80 kilometres (50 miles) on guided float trips, which are an ideal way to get away from the crowds, small though they are. Some of the best fishing on the Elk River actually takes place in August and September, when the cutthroat trout are beefed up and hungry. In some years, it can be absolutely red hot in September, and you'll have the river virtually to yourself.

Cutthroat trout are sleepy-heads, and it isn't necessary to get on the water at first light. Mountain streams cool during the night, and it's best to wait until the water warms up by mid-morning, which is when the daily action kicks into gear. It picks up even more during the afternoon until the sun sets. Some of the best dry fly fishing occurs right after sun down, when the winds are usually calm and secretive trout

An inflatable raft will get you to some out-of-the-way places on the Elk River.

move into prime feeding areas in shallow backwaters out of the main current in the gurgling Elk River.

The Elk River has many different, rather unique sections that can be a challenge to the itinerant fly fisher: from experiencing "the vortex" at a mountain pass near Morrissey, which makes casting almost impossible at times; to the serenity of the headwaters where trout are still naïve enough to strike at just about any offering; to the evening rises for tiny emergers in the backwaters of the lower Elk River near Fernie.

Fernie is the fly fishing epicentre for trips on the Elk River and its tributaries. The city is probably best known for world-class ski vacations but has really hit the fly fishing charts over the past decade despite controversial classified waters regulations. These regulations came into effect several years ago in response to rising concerns from locals about escalating non-resident

traffic on the Elk River. While the regulations have upset some anglers, others view the changes as being positive and well worth the added expense.

Fernie is a picturesque city along Highway 3 in southeastern British Columbia. It is the regional centre in the East Kootenays on the western border of the Crowsnest Pass. It boasts fine accommodations and dining and has several fly fishing shops and guiding businesses, such as The Kootenay Fly Shop and Guiding Company and Elk River Guiding Company. It's the closest thing in Canada to Ennis, Montana, as a hotbed of fly fishing junkies.

For camping and RV enthusiasts, Mount Fernie Provincial Park is located 3 kilometres (2 miles) south of Fernie along Highway 3. I always enjoy a day on the water capped off by an evening meal and cool ale at The Bridge Bistro on the bank of the Elk River in Fernie; the Curry Bowl is another of my favourite restaurants. The scenery along the Elk River is second to none, and even though Highway 3 parallels the river for much of its length, you'd think you were deep in the Canadian wilderness; it's that quiet and serene.

Guided trips are an indulgence but well worth the expense if you want to reach some out-of-the-way places on the Elk River. Such trips begin with a rendezvous with a local guide at your accommodations or a local fly shop followed by a drive to an access site along the river. Trips usually begin at 9:00 AM and often last until late in the evening. The guide does all the work, rowing and manoeuvring a Mackenzie-style drift boat or inflatable raft to position it for casting by the sports. Trips customarily include a shore lunch, some of which are a gourmet's delight. Beverages are also provided as part of the package. Typically, you'll stop at promising pools and runs along the river during the trip to do some

walk-and-wade fishing. Most local guides are knowledgeable fly fishermen and can provide some good advice to novices and veteran fly fishers alike.

You do not have to book a guided trip, however, to enjoy fishing on the Elk River and its tributaries. Many anglers enjoy walk-and-wade fishing or drift the river in pontoon boats and do very well by themselves. There's good access to the Elk River at various bridge crossings along Highway 3, and most tributaries can be accessed by mining and logging roads. One advantage of a guided trip into the backcountry is that the guides are knowledgeable about logging truck traffic, and this is a safety precaution to keep in mind. On another note, bears are often sighted in the Elk River drainage, and anglers should take normal precautions to avoid encounters with grizzly bears, in particular. Be sure to carry bear spray.

Shore lunches are a gourmet's delight and a highlight of a guided trip.

The Fernie area tends to be hot and dry during summer, although thunderstorms are common and gusty winds can interfere with fly casting as the day warms up. Fly casters must change their casting trajectory when winds become an issue, especially near "the vortex" in the vicinity of Morrissey (between Fernie and Elko), where wind gusts are quite common during summer. Another option is to use an 8-weight fly rod and use the water to load your fly line prior to casting to counteract occasional strong winds.

While fly fishing for cutthroat trout doesn't have to be technical, there are some days when you'll be scratching your head to come up with workable patterns and other days when you'll really have to stretch your skills and knowledge to get hook-ups. Once, on a guided trip on the Fording River, our guide went through more than two dozen patterns even though trout were rising steadily as he went through his fly

box before he hit on the ticket—a Grey Wulff dry fly—after which we couldn't keep the fish off. What I enjoy most about fly fishing the Elk River and its tributaries is that it consistently produces on dry flies. I've never had to resort to nymphs or streamers; dry fly fishing has been that reliable. If there's one go-to guide fly, it would probably be a Chernobyl Ant, which is deadly most days, followed by large Stimulators with orange or yellow bodies.

On a typical day, I'll start with various search patterns if there's no obvious surface action—for example, large attractor flies such as the Madame X, Turk's Tarantula and Chernobyl Ant, or various Stimulators, one of which will usually get a rise. Other standby fly patterns are Parachute Adams, Elk Hair Caddis and various Humpy and Hopper patterns, especially in late summer, fished up tight against the stream bank. I like to skate attractor patterns, which hungry trout usually find

An Elk River tributary cutthroat trout.

Pinpoint casting is an essential skill when fishing from a Mackenzie-style drift boat.

irresistible: cast into a promising lair, then retrieve the fly in short, erratic strips, dancing the fly over the water. I generally fish other patterns in a dead drift and brace myself for a hook-up. I've never been handicapped dry fly fishing on the Elk River or any of its tributaries. However, if you want to fish with nymphs and streamers, I'm sure you'll have good results with various bead head patterns, and weighted Woolly Buggers in particular. Mend your line upstream as often as necessary when using a dead drift, and use lots of fly floatant.

My personal preference when fishing for cutthroats is a 6-weight fly rod with floating line and a 9-foot leader with matching tippet. You usually don't have to make long casts, and generally the shorter the cast the better so you can better manage your fly line. It is important, though, to make accurate casts because cutthroat trout often rest in pocket water associated with otherwise turbulent stretches, which can be challenging to fish.

Trout can be almost anywhere in the Elk River, but the hot spots are usually under foam lines in pools, at the intersection of seams in runs and in pocket water along the stream bank. During walk-and-wade trips, make a habit of breaking the water into an imaginary grid and cast into each part of the grid before moving on. You'll be surprised at where you'll find trout, which are often right at your feet. When fly fishing from a drift boat, the rule of thumb is to cast in a downstream direction or sideways using a straight-line or reach cast with an upstream mend. Let the fly float in a dead drift. Pinpoint casting is essential, so practice up before you fork over your hard-earned cash for a guided trip.

British Columbia's Elk River and its tributaries really are a Mecca for cutthroat trout and a dry fly fishing delight on a lightweight fly rod. You don't have to travel to exotic places such as New Zealand or Patagonia to enjoy some of the world's best fly fishing; it's right in your backyard!

If You Go

Fishing Regulations: The Elk River drainage is located in Region 4—Kootenay in the British Columbia Freshwater Fishing Regulations Synopsis. No fishing is permitted in any stream in Region 4 from April 1 to June 14. Only single barbless hooks are permitted during the rest of the year. The Elk River and its tributaries are designated as Class II Classified Waters and require a supplemental Classified Waters Licence in addition to a freshwater fishing licence. In addition, non-residents must book time on classified streams on a first come, first served basis. Anglers should check the regulations to ensure they're in compliance with the law when fishing in these waters.

Fly Fishing Adventure at the Pitt River Lodge, BC

At the crack of the bear banger, the medium-sized black bear took off like a racehorse! Nick Didlick, my fishing guide, had made a perfect shot with his flare gun—the cartridge exploded just above Smoky. The bear bolted upstream, then stopped and looked back to see what caused the commotion before Nick sent another flare his way that really put him into high gear. It's all in a day fishing on a coastal stream in beautiful British Columbia…where we saw four black bears that day, as well as a huge Roosevelt bull elk with his harem of cows. I was fly fishing on the Pitt River out of the Pitt River Lodge in the Coastal Range, a little peace of heaven on earth. Greater Vancouver, with a population of about 2.3 million residents, was just over the mountains. Yes, it was hard to believe that a wilderness fly fishing trip was even possible so close to this large urban centre.

Fly fishing with inflatable rafts on the Pitt River, British Columbia.

Nick Didlick throwing line on the Pitt River with a Spey rod.

The Pitt River is a large, freestone river that rushes towards Pitt Lake and then the Pacific Ocean. It's nestled between Garibaldi Provincial Park, Pinecone Burke Park and Golden Ears Provincial Park in what goes for "Sea to Sky Country" in the parlance of Tourism BC. The Pitt River Lodge features year-round fishing for salmon, trout, steelhead and even white sturgeon. The runs vary seasonally, with sockeye and coho peak runs in September and October, respectively. The Pitt River is especially renowned for its excellent fly fishing for rare bull trout; it is one of the few streams where a fly angler can target bull trout during a fly fishing trip with an expectation to catch a trophy fish.

My hosts were Lee MacGregor and Danny Gerak, who have been running the Pitt River Lodge since October 2000. Lee hails from Nelson, BC, while Danny's home is in nearby New Westminster. Only catch-and-release fishing is allowed on the Pitt River,

and 95 percent of the clientele are fly fishers who hail from around the world. In 2012, the lodge went totally fly fishing. I was paired up with Sven-Olaf Rahband-Dula, a banker from Frankfurt, Germany, who had earlier fished with Nick and was back to try his luck once again. Sven is a great guy, an ardent fly fisher who fished exclusively with a Spey rod while I used a single-handled 8-weight fly rod.

I flew into the Abbotsford International Airport and then travelled by car to Grant Narrows Regional Park, where Danny met me for a boat trip to the far end of Pitt Lake. From there we took a vehicle on an old logging road to the lodge. The Pitt River Lodge reminded me of a country inn in Canada's Maritimes; I regretted not bringing my slippers and a housecoat! It was a full-service lodge featuring comfortable rooms with linen service, showers (even a bathtub), indoor toilets, a lounge with internet and TV, a bar and games

Pitt River Lodge.

room. The lodge routine had us up for breakfast at 7:30 AM, on the water shortly after, lunch on the river, and back for dinner at 7:00 PM. The food was excellent. During my stay, dinners featured rib-eye steaks, curried chicken, baked salmon and ribs, with all the fixings, served with wine; breakfasts were equally tasty and nutritious.

The lodge uses self-draining inflatable rafts to float the Pitt River. Clients disembark and fish promising holding water along the way. It's not safe to fish from the rafts because of all the logjams and sweepers. All guests are fitted with life jackets for their safety. The Pitt River is fly fishing friendly. There's lots of casting room. I think I only got caught up a couple of times on streamside vegetation. The gravel and cobble is clean and not slippery. You don't actually have to bring any fishing gear—the lodge can fit you up with chest waders, wading boots and quality fly fishing rods and reels.

I very much enjoyed fly fishing with Nick Didlick, who's one of the best guides in the region, on top of being an excellent

photographer. He invented a fly pattern several years ago called Kelsey's Hope, which is a freshwater coho salmon pattern of note. Another one of Nick's go-to flies is called a Christmas Tree and was ideal for the fast water, and one of the better producers. The usual fly fishing drill is to cast

Nick Didlick with his original Kelsey's Hope fly pattern.

across and down, using a sink tip line with a short 15- to 20-pound monofilament leader rigged with various streamers. Fly fishers fish the streamer in a dead drift, mending if necessary, then strip on the retrieve once it's finished its swing. Nick suggested stepping along methodically, fairly quickly, through holding water and cautioned that strikes might be subtle in the cold water.

During that October, trip conditions weren't exactly ideal for fly fishing because there had been two days of heavy rain the week before I arrived, when the river blew out. It was still running high and a bit cloudy my first day on the water. It dropped 1.5 feet overnight and continued to drop until I left. Trout and salmon do not like unstable water levels, and fishing is usually off until flows are stable. The water was quite cold: a steady 8° C during my trip. Nonetheless, Sven and I enjoyed some

great fly fishing for bull trout, in particular, and I also caught cutthroats and rainbows, as well as coho salmon.

Typically, I got off to a good start each morning with hook-ups on bull trout, cutthroats or rainbows before 10:00 AM and then had to work for my fish until later in the day when the bite picked up once again. The area abounds with all manner of avian predators (e.g., bald eagles, kingfishers, blue herons, mergansers, osprey), which likely keep the fish on alert during the midday period, along with occasional seals that swim up river from the Pacific Ocean.

Starting in 2012, anglers had a real treat in store for them when Lee and Danny celebrated a grand opening of the new Pitt River Lodge, which is now being used for overflow purposes. It's situated upriver from where the original lodge is located, with eight guests per week, and is for fly

The author with a Pitt River bull trout.

fishers only. It's an eye-popping log building with a breath-taking, panoramic view of the Pitt River valley. The new lodge features a stunning interior with spacious, upscale rooms. It's one of the nicest fishing lodges I've ever seen, with all the amenities of a grand hotel and then some. I can hardly wait to return and once again fly fish the pristine waters of the Pitt River.

If You Go

Fishing Regulations: You'll need a BC Freshwater Fishing Licence, which can be obtained online. Several types of licences are available for non-residents of BC.

If time permits, you might want to try fly fishing for salmon on the Fraser River near Chilliwack prior to going into the lodge or upon your return. Check out Great River Fishing Adventures for details.

BC's Skeena River Tributaries: Steelhead Battle, with Coho as a Bonus

Fly anglers get all teary eyed when talk swings to fly fishing for romantic steelhead, but the unheralded coho salmon should get a higher rating because they are challenging to catch by fly fishing. One of the world's top destinations where you can catch both steelhead and coho during the same trip is in the Skeena River drainage out of Terrace, British Columbia.

As the sun dropped below the peaks of a coastal mountain range, it felt like I was in the bottom of the ninth inning. I was on a fly fishing adventure on a torrential tributary of the Skeena River in BC in late October. I'd been wading in 5° C water for the better part of the day. I was trying to shake my disappointment after having hooked and lost a couple of large steelhead trout earlier on in the day. I wouldn't go home skunked because I'd landed my first-ever steelhead the day before, but I couldn't help but feel a bit melancholy

Fishing guide Greg Buck in an inflatable raft on a Skeena River tributary.

The author with a steelhead from a Skeena River tributary.

as I made yet another across and down cast into a promising run. Sky Richard, my Nicholas Dean Lodge fishing guide, coached me to angle my cast farther downstream to get a bit longer of a drift, and not to strip the line until it completely straightened out in the current.

I'm the first to admit that I'd suffered from a bit of stage fright during this trip—which was my first for steelhead—similar to the butterflies I'd experienced during my first trip for Atlantic salmon on the famed Miramichi River in New Brunswick. But when the chips are down, an itinerant fly fisherman has to stay positive and fish with the resolve that every cast could pay dividends.

Time stopped when I felt a solid strike, and a huge steelhead broke the water. It rocketed from the run in an explosion of water in a frenzied attempt to throw the hook.

Once again, that magic moment had arrived when patience and perseverance pay off with a fine fish on the end of my line. As the chrome-sided beauty peeled off yards of line, breaking the water several more times, I could relate to the Nirvana of catching this iconic wild salmonid of Canada's west coast. What a thrill! When the sleek trout was eventually landed for a quick photo, I had a smile as big the Cheshire cat, and I felt a warm glow of satisfaction despite the chill in the air. Not 10 minutes later I would experience another high when I landed another fine steelhead. How could fishing get any better?

For a fly fisherman, Canada features at least two dream trips—Atlantic salmon and steelhead trout—actually maybe four if you add huge Arctic char and lake trout. I was now the wiser after having completed my grand slam on one of the tributaries of

Dustin Kovacvich with a coho salmon taken on a fly.

the storied Skeena River. I'd risen to the challenge of fly fishing for steelhead (landing several over the course of two days), which made my late season trip all the more interesting and exciting.

Back to the rhetorical question, how could such a trip get any better? Well, actually it did on my final day out with Dustin Kovacvich, Nicholas Dean Lodge manager and head guide, on a fly fishing outing in search of coho salmon. I'd racked up a good score on day one of my trip while fishing with a veteran guide, Greg Buck, before targeting steelhead trout for the next couple of days, having landed several fine coho as well as a number of Dolly Varden and bull trout during the outing with Greg. This was my first stream fly fishing trip for coho salmon, although I had taken them previously in the Pacific Ocean when

fly fishing out of Weight West Marine Resort at Tofino on Vancouver Island—a totally different and hairy fly fishing experience.

Dustin Kovacvich is an all-around outdoorsman who's at home in the bush; plus he's an expert fly fisherman who has the goods on fly fishing for coho. He's a giant of a man, standing 6 feet, 6 inches tall, which gives him an advantage when scouting for fish. He also knows how to take to the chase when fishing for coho, which are a migratory species that move about the tributaries of the Skeena River. There's an old saying that you should save the best for last, and on this trip maybe it came to fruition. I'm abashed to say how many coho I actually caught, but it was well into the double digits thanks to Dustin's excellent guiding skills and his local knowledge. I'm not exaggerating about my catch. I'm certain I could have easily landed at least 40 coho salmon had that been my objective. In addition to catching them by sight fishing, I took over a dozen from some fish traps Dustin suggested targeting. One place in particular was a serious honey hole where I caught many coho in the 10- to 15-pound range.

Nicholas Dean Lodge has been in operation since 2004 and originally went by the name Nicholas Dean Outfitters. Its headquarters are in Terrace, a thoroughly modern city in the heart of BC's coastal rainforest. The lodge operations manager is Chad Black, an experienced fly fishing guide who hails from Fergus, Ontario, and joined the management team in 2007. Chad has been in the fishing industry since he was a teenager. He says the most enjoyable part of his job is interacting with clients from all over the world and living his dream of being part a grand fly fishing experience.

Although I stayed at the Yellow Cedar Lodge during my trip, guests now stay at the Pioneer Fishing Lodge. Chad Black advised that they've moved operations from Yellow Cedar to Pioneer Fishing Lodge now, and for the most part, no longer work with Yellow Cedar Lodge. He says they're still on good terms with them and have a couple of groups who stay there each year who are good friends with the lodge owners, but aside from this, all of Nicholas Dean Lodge's clientele now stay at Pioneer Fishing Lodge.

When fly fishing for steelhead on the smaller tributaries, you'll drift downstream in self-draining, inflatable rafts, stopping at promising holding water along the way. Don't even think about floating these rivers on your own; they're Class 3 and 4 rivers suitable for expert oarsmen only. Many stretches feature numerous large, standing waves, hairpin turns and generally rough, turbulent waters. Be prepared to hang onto your seat, and get ready for a wash from time to time.

Fishing guide Sky Richard with an inflatable raft on a Skeena River tributary.

Many anglers use Spey rods when fishing for steelhead. I used an 8-weight Orvis Hydros rod rigged with a Rio shooting line and various shooting heads, with 3-foot, 20-pound leaders. The guides will change the shooting heads as required to get into the strike zone and can supply go-to flies. Recommended streamer flies for steelhead are the Candy Cane, Nathan's Magic and Morris Trailer Trash Nightshade; also recommended are Bomber dry flies. I'm confident that large, foam-fly attractor patterns will catch steelhead early in autumn. Cast across and down, fish the streamer in a dead drift, let it go through a full swing in the current, then strip the fly during your retrieve.

When fly fishing for coho salmon on the larger tributaries, guides use jet boats. Leave this to the pros who know how to read water; don't try it yourself or you'll likely end up hospitalized and dealing with a backcountry wreck. Coastal mountain streams are subject to a wide range of flows; they're often braided with shallow channels, numerous sweepers, logjams and swift currents, and they are no place for amateurs.

Dustin said Spey rods are a liability when fly fishing for coho. He suggested using 8- or 9-weight rods with a shooting line and shooting heads with short 20-pound leaders. Coho are not leader shy. He favours several bitch streamers, as did Greg, featuring pink, blue and chartreuse colours. Both Greg and Dustin said that short "cat-and-mouse" strips were the ticket for coho, and they were correct. While I wasn't used to fly casting with shooting heads, I caught on quickly. I did have a bit of trouble with my back cast when pitching the large streamers the guides favoured, which had large,

A coho salmon caught fly fishing.

tungsten heads. They're not aerodynamic at all. Coho don't feed when in fresh water; rather, they chase flies and likely strike them out of aggression. They'll hold in slack water and especially frog water (i.e., small areas of still water), close up against the stream bank, away from the main current. Accurate casts are paramount to being successful, and this is where a single-handed fly rod comes into play.

Dustin spent a lot of time talking to me about the best times and places to fish various species of salmon and steelhead on the Skeena River and its tributaries. I went in late October because I wanted to double up on steelhead trout and coho. You may want to fly fish for other species of salmon or at different times for steelhead, all of which are doable. Nicholas Dean Lodge will provide you with details on how to prepare for your trip. Rain gear is a must, and the guides will suggest that you practice fly casting before your trip so you're up to speed before you arrive.

The Skeena River and its tributaries boast some of the best fishing for salmon and steelhead in the world. The Canadian record Chinook salmon was caught in the Skeena River in 1959 and weighed 92.5 pounds. About 25 local rivers can be fished out of Nicholas Dean Lodge, so if one river is blown out there are always other options; the lodge has rod-day allocations adequate for all manner of itinerant fly fishers.

Was there one special moment during the time I spent fly fishing on the Skeena River tributaries? Was it my first coho salmon or wild steelhead trout on a fly rod? Was it the double headers on both steelhead and coho that my fishing buddy, Shaul Kuper of Toronto, and I experienced on day one and day two of the trip, respectively? Was it the serenity of fishing in magnificent streams in a coastal

The author with a male coho salmon from a Skeena River tributary.

rainforest? It was all of these moments combined with the exhilaration of some wild, white-water floats and jet boat rides in one of the most spectacular areas in Canada—a memorable life experience.

If You Go

The season starts on March 15 for spring steelhead and closes on November 15. From June to November there are numerous packages for fly fishing for Chinook, steelhead and other species of salmon. Their home base is in Terrace; however, guiding takes place in a 300-kilometre (200-mile) radius in all directions, including some "off-the-wall" adventure experiences. Contact Nicholas Dean Lodge for a customized trip.

Edmonton's Top 10 Fly Fishing Day Trips

1. East Pit Lake

Species available: rainbow trout

Nearest communities: Spruce Grove, Stony Plain, Wabamun

East Pit Lake is an old TransAlta strip mine pit that has been reclaimed and is being managed as a stocked trout pond. The lake is situated on a 126-hectare (312-acre) conservation property west of Edmonton. Take Highway 16 to Exit 324 (directly north of Wabamun) and go 1.6 kilometres north to the parking area on the west side of the road. The access site at the lake is managed as a day-use recreation area with hiking trails. The lake has produced trophy-size rainbow trout, especially after it was initially stocked, partly because the trout grew large in the previously barren water, and also because access has always been limited to foot traffic only.

This lake is probably best fished with a belly boat, although casting from shore is popular. Chironomid fishing is productive, or try small bait fish imitation patterns such as black and olive Woolly Buggers as well as water boatmen, and backswimmers in autumn.

The lake is open year-round. At the time of writing, the daily trout limit is five. Fly fishermen should source the Alberta Conservation Association discovery guide for maps and details on publicly accessible land for hunting, fishing and hiking in Alberta, including East Pit Lake.

2. Maligne Lake

Species available: brook trout, rainbow trout

Nearest communities: Hinton, Jasper town site

Maligne Lake is located in Jasper National Park and is favourite destination for Edmonton fly fishers. Travel west on

East Pit Lake pothole fishery.

Highway 16; take a secondary road just before the Jasper town site to Maligne Lake. Yes, it's a long day trip but well worth the effort. No gas motorboats are allowed on the lake, only electric motors. Boat rentals are available at Curly Phillip's Boathouse. Guided trips can be booked in Jasper.

Fly fishing for trout involves two basic approaches: (1) fishing with eye-catching streamers such as the Little Rainbow, Little Brook Trout, Mickey Finn and Double Shrimp, by trolling and power stripping; and (2) fishing with bead head nymphs and chironomids over prime feeding areas off points and in bays. The fish are not everywhere; you'll have to search them out and try both techniques to be successful.

Maligne Lake is open from May 16 to September 30. Note that the Maligne Lake outlet and Maligne River—the portion including the part of Maligne Lake within a 100-metre (330-foot) radius of a point in the middle of the Maligne River where it leaves Maligne Lake, to a point 420 metres

Maligne Lake, Jasper National Park.

(1400 feet) downstream from the Maligne Lake outlet bridge—is closed year round. At the time of writing, the limit on brook trout and rainbow trout is two fish daily, regardless of species.

Because Maligne Lake is such an outstanding fishery, a whole section is devoted to this lake. See page 146.

A rainbow trout from Maligne Lake, Jasper National Park.

3. McLeod River

Species available: Arctic grayling, brook trout, bull trout, mountain whitefish, rainbow trout

Nearest communities: Cadomin, Edson, Hinton

The upper McLeod River is a popular fly fishing destination in the Alberta foothills near Edson, south of Highway 16. The river originates near Cadomin and is a tributary of the Athabasca River. It features Arctic grayling, brook trout, bull trout, mountain whitefish and rainbow trout in its headwaters, with walleye being found in the lower reaches downstream of Highway 16.

The usual patterns will catch trout: attractor flies such as Orange and Yellow Stimulators, Turks Tarantula, Madame X and the Chernobyl Ant. Bead head nymphs will catch all the species, including Arctic

A McLeod River Arctic grayling.

grayling. Streamers work best for bull trout (for which there is a zero limit)—cone head Woolly Buggers and Muddler Minnows are effective bully patterns fished with a sink tip line.

The regulations vary from one section of the river to another, so check the "Alberta Guide to Sportfishing Regulations" for season dates and catch limits.

A bull trout from the Athabasca River, near the McLeod River.

Muir Lake anglers.

4. Muir Lake

Species available: rainbow trout, brown trout

Nearest communities: Edmonton, Stony Plain, Spruce Grove

Muir Lake is the pet project of several Edmonton fishing clubs: Edmonton Trout Fishing Club, Northern Lights Fly Tiers TU Chapter and Edmonton Old-timers Fishing Club. The grand opening of this rejuvenated fishery occurred in May 2004, after two lake aerators were installed and a walk-of-fame and education centre was completed at the public access site provided by Parkland County. Travel west on Highway 16 from Edmonton, turn north on Highway 779 to Township Road 540, turn east, then turn south on Range Road 275 and drive for 3.2 kilometres until you reach the lake.

Several patterns will catch fish at Muir Lake: chironomids, Woolly Buggers, water boatmen, backswimmers, the bead head Pheasant Tail, bead head Prince Nymph and bead head shrimp. Trout in excess of 18 inches are being caught, and sizes are on the rise.

Muir Lake is stocked annually. The lake is subject to special regulations: it is open May 1 to October 31 with a trout limit of one over 20 inches, and a bait ban; it is closed from November 1 to April 30 (there is no ice fishing while the lake is being aerated).

5. North Ram River

Species available: cutthroat trout

Nearest communities: Nordegg, Rocky Mountain House

The North Ram River is located west of Rocky Mountain House, south of Nordegg in the foothills of Alberta's eastern slopes. While it's a fairly long drive for a day's fishing, it's feasible to leave Edmonton early in the morning and get in a good day on the water before returning home—I've done it. Take Highway 22 south of Edmonton to Rocky Mountain House; drive west on Highway 11 until you reach the Forestry Trunk Road (Secondary Road 734) and head south until you reach the forestry campsite beside the North Ram River. The river was originally barren of fish. Stockings of west slope cutthroat trout in 1961 and 1971 took, and the North Ram River now boasts one of Alberta's premier cutthroat fisheries. Jim Wagner, provincial fisheries management spokesperson advised, "There is no indication of where the fish came from, but given the date, I would guess they were from the Federal [National] Parks and most likely Pickle Jar or Marvel Lakes."

Cutthroat trout can be taken on dry fly patterns, nymphs and streamers. Start with search patterns such as Stimulators or a Chernobyl Ant to locate positive trout, and if these patterns fail, then follow up with bead head nymphs such as the Pheasant Tail or Prince Nymph. If you still don't have any action, switch to streamers, such as a bead head Woolly Bugger.

Fly fishing is best during mid-July and August, once the river shapes up following the spring runoff, until mid-September.

The North Ram River.

A North Ram River cutthroat trout.

Mountain streams cool down at night, and fishing doesn't pick up until late morning when the water temperature rises—there's no reason to speed all the way down from Edmonton because the morning bite is typically slow.

At the time of writing, the North Ram River has a zero limit and a bait ban. The open season is from June 16 to October 31.

6. North Raven River (Stauffer Creek)
Species available: brook trout, brown trout

Nearest communities: Caroline, Red Deer, Rocky Mountain House

The North Raven River is located in west-central Alberta southeast of Rocky Mountain House. If travelling from Edmonton, go south on Highway 2, then west on Highway 11 and turn south on Highway 761. Check out the Alberta Conservation Association discovery guide online for information regarding the public access site on the North Raven River.

The North Raven River has long been a go-to stream for Edmonton fly fishers; it's one of Alberta's top spring creek fisheries. However, it can be a heartbreaker for advanced fly fishers and novices alike. It's difficult to fish because of willows along the stream banks and skittish trout in the clear water. The brown trout population, in particular, appears to fluctuate. It was first

Typical stream bank cover on the North Raven River.

A North Raven River brook trout.

7. North Saskatchewan River

Species available: goldeye/mooneye, mountain whitefish, northern pike, walleye

Nearest communities: Edmonton, Devon, Spruce Grove, Stony Plain

The North Saskatchewan River flows through Edmonton and is the nearest river for local fly fishing enthusiasts. It's a large river best fished from a jet boat, but many spots within the city afford easy access for a day's outing. While most trips take place upstream of Edmonton in the vicinity of Devon and farther upstream towards Drayton Valley, there has been a steady growth in fishing within the city proper over the past several years.

Edmonton has one of the largest urban parks in North America, with an excellent series of day use areas and public access points adjacent to the North Saskatchewan River. The City of Edmonton Community Services Department has published a "River Recreation Guide" that features the locations of key public access points. This handy brochure is a must-have document for fly fishers. Upstream of Edmonton,

stocked with brown trout in the 1930s. Alberta Conservation Association long-term studies indicate that there was a general trend of increased abundance of brown trout from 1973 until 1985, followed by a reduction in abundance but increase in biomass in 1995, suggesting there were fewer fish but of a larger size in the 1995 catch. Both the abundance and biomass of brook trout appear to have declined over the same time frame. From 1995 to 2005, a general trend of increased brook trout and decreased brown trout abundance and biomass is evident.

Fly fishers can anticipate small, dark stoneflies followed by Skwalas in spring; Blue Winged Olives, March Browns, Green Drakes during summer; caddis towards autumn. Edmonton Trout Fishing Club members opt for a "Stauffer Special," which may have been originally tied by the late Lloyd Shea in the 1950s.

Check the "Alberta Guide to Sportfishing Regulations" for fishing regulations. A bait ban is in effect year-round.

Getting ready for a trip on the North Saskatchewan River.

A walleye from the North Saskatchewan River.

most access is at bridge crossings or across private land, where anglers must obtain permission to fish.

Goldeye/mooneye are summer residents, arriving in late spring as the runoff subsides and leaving for points downstream in late summer. Goldeye/mooneye are very forgiving and can be taken on full back and attractor patterns, with foam flies being dynamite. They put up a spirited battle on a 4-weight fly rod and can be caught in abundance throughout the river. It's not unusual to catch goldeye/mooneye in the 12-inch–plus range, lots of them.

Northern pike distribution is spotty throughout the river; they're not overly abundant, but there are trophy-size pike to be had with streamers, large deceivers being the best bet. Search backwaters for large pike.

Walleye are abundant in the river, particularly above Edmonton but also within the city limits, and they can be taken with streamers such as dark Woolly Buggers. Walleye tend to favour select pools, where they congregate during summer, but in autumn, all bets are off below Devon as they move to overwintering pools upstream and downstream. There's good walleye fishing in the river, with trophy fish caught each year.

The odd brown trout is taken upstream of Edmonton, and while mountain whitefish are fairly abundant throughout the river, they're not targeted by anglers to a large degree.

The river is open all year from Highway 22/39 (Drayton Valley) downstream to the Alberta/Saskatchewan border. Check the "Alberta Guide to Sportfishing Regulations" for details.

8. Red Deer River

Species available: brown trout, goldeye, mountain whitefish, walleye

Nearest communities: Innisfail, Red Deer

The Red Deer River is a popular destination for Edmonton-area fly fishers, who target brown trout and mountain whitefish, in particular, downstream of Glennifer Lake (Dickson Dam) to the city of Red Deer. The Red Deer River features floats on various sections downstream of the Dickson Dam to Red Deer through a picturesque prairie landscape, wherever access is available adjacent to various secondary roads. It is a river that's unnervingly quiet compared with other similar float trips, very peaceful and relaxing in a pastoral setting. Because of the regulated flows below Glennifer Lake, floats are feasible from mid-June through to October in the tail waters below the Dickson Dam.

It was the controversial transplants of catchable-size brown trout from the Bow River to the Red Deer River in 1991 and 1992 that most likely kick-started the brown trout fishery, but the brown trout population in the Red Deer River has had its ups and downs due to floods in 1995 and 2005 in particular—the latter year being a complete write-off for fishing. Brown trout redd counts are still low compared with historic levels because the population is slow to recover from these devastating floods.

The number of brown trout in the Red Deer River is not large, but it does boast bragging-size trophies greater than

Float trips are available on the Red Deer River.

A Red Deer River brown trout.

22 inches, which are a major draw. It appears the best way to catch brown trout is by snout hunting and then targeting the fish with dry flies; streamers would be a second choice if there's no surface action, albeit a long shot under most circumstances. Why? It appears that brown trout occupy rather specific niches in the Red Deer River; they're not everywhere, but rather they situate themselves near undercut banks, root balls and the like. The summer hatches are of pale morning duns, caddis and brown drakes, with caddis in autumn.

The Red Deer River has long been a go-to spot for anglers in search of mountain whitefish, which are most common upstream of Red Deer to Dickson Dam.

While a Golden Stone or Brown Hackle would be my choice for mountain whitefish in summer, I'd opt for a bead head Pheasant Tail or Prince Nymph during autumn, all fished with a sink tip line.

The river is lousy with goldeye, which can be caught on attractor patterns and various hopper patterns, as well as on many wet flies. If the action on brown trout is slow, goldeye will more than make up for it with nonstop rises during the entire day all summer long. While walleye are present in the Red Deer River, I've never heard of fly fishers targeting them.

Check the angling regulations for open seasons on the Red Deer River, which has different closed seasons for various reaches.

Spring Lake pothole fishery.

9. *Spring (Cottage) Lake*
Species available: rainbow trout, yellow perch

Nearest communities: Edmonton, Spruce Grove, Stony Plain

Spring (Cottage) Lake is the home water of the Edmonton Trout Fishing Club and is stocked annually with rainbow trout. Access has been an issue over the past few years, but it appears as though the Village of Spring Lake is supportive of maintaining public access at the local campground and by various walking trails. Travel 5 kilometres west of Stony Plain on Highway 16 to Beach Corner, then south for 5 kilometres. Members of the Edmonton Trout Fishing Club gain access through two lots that they've owned for many years. The first, at 675 Lakeshore Drive, is an empty lot with a locked gate through which members have access by signing out a key from the Property Chairperson. This gate allows drive-through access from the road to the club shelter, pier and boat storage area. Boats are stored at members' own risk. The second, at 670 Lakeshore Drive, is open with a grassy area adjacent to the road where members may camp. From here there are steps leading down to the club's shelter, swings and washrooms. Anglers can do their part to keep public access open by picking up litter and following club property rules.

Popular flies are bead head Woolly Buggers, chironomids, damselfly nymphs, full backs and water boatmen during summer, and backswimmers in autumn.

Spring (Cottage) Lake is open year-round. At the time of writing, the trout limit is five.

10. Star Lake

Species available: rainbow trout

Nearest communities: Edmonton, Spruce Grove, Stony Plain

Star Lake is a pothole lake fishery west of Edmonton. Go approximately 15 kilometres west of Stony Plain on Highway 16 to Highway 770 and then south for about 7 kilometres, and then another 3 kilometres west. There's an old public access site on Star Lake. Typical of other potholes in the area, water levels have been receding over the past several years, which increases the probability of both winterkill and summerkill.

The lake has a reputation for spotty fishing but also for some trophy-sized fish. The usual go-to patterns for pothole lakes in the Edmonton area will catch rainbows: leeches, chironomids, water boatmen and backswimmers.

A Star Lake rainbow trout.

Star Lake is open year-round, with a limit of five trout at the time of writing.

There are several other popular pothole lakes similar to Star, East Pit, Muir and Spring lakes that are close to Edmonton: Carson, Chickakoo, Dolberg, Goldeye, Hasse, Lower Chain, Millers, Mitchell and Salters lakes, to name a few.

Hasse Lake pothole fishery.

Spirit Island in Maligne Lake, Jasper National Park.

Alberta's Magnificent Maligne Lake

If ever there was a misnomer, it has to be Maligne Lake. The lake takes its name from the French word *maligne*, meaning "malignant" or "wicked." To the contrary, Maligne Lake should have been named something more descriptive along the lines of Lac Magnifique. The lake was well known to the First Nations of the area, who knew it as *Chaba Imne* (Beaver Lake). It's the largest lake in Jasper National Park, and it has long been a hot spot for fly fishing enthusiasts. I've fished it many times, and it never fails to disappoint me.

There's no doubt that it gets some of its notoriety because the Alberta record rainbow trout was caught there in 1980. This monster 'bow weighed 20 pounds, 4 ounces and is on display in the Jasper Park Lodge. Don't get your hopes up that you might catch a fish of this size anytime soon at Maligne Lake—a 10-pound rainbow trout would be exceptional these days. However, some large eastern brook trout have been caught in Maligne Lake, just under the current Alberta record at 12 pounds, 14 ounces, which was caught in Pine Lake in Wood Buffalo National Park in 1967. My bet is that the next Alberta record brook trout will be caught from Maligne Lake's eye-catching turquoise waters.

Actually, you don't even have to catch any trout, and you'll still have a great experience on Maligne Lake amid the grandeur of the Alberta Rockies. It's one of the most picturesque lakes in Alberta, and its storied Spirit Island is one of the most photographed landscapes in Canada. The drive from Highway 16 to Maligne Lake is a serpentine paved road that features breathtaking panoramas and often wildlife. I've seen timber wolves along this road several times, as well as black bears, mule deer, elk and bighorn sheep. It's always a treat just driving to the lake, one that always gives me a Rocky Mountain high.

I wouldn't say that there's actually a "best" time to fly fish for trout in Maligne Lake. You can and should expect to catch fish throughout the open season. Brook trout fishing generally picks up when the water temperature is within their preferred range of 7–16° C. They seek temperatures below 20° C when surface waters warm up. Fishing for rainbows is best when the water temperature is 10–21° C. Be sure to pack your thermometer, check surface water temperatures and adjust your fishing strategy accordingly.

My advice is to fish from a freighter canoe rigged with an electric motor. Experienced boaters take a spare electric motor and extra batteries because the lake is quite large and you'll do a lot of travelling while you chase trout during the course of a day. If you've ever tried to row a freighter canoe on a lake, then you'll know why a spare motor and extra batteries are recommended. The drill is to take the chase to trout by trolling between promising bays and shoals that are scattered along the

Freighter canoes are recommended for fishing Maligne Lake.

lake's shoreline. A 5- to 6-weight rod rigged with a full sink line and a long leader is the ticket when trolling. I recommend fluorocarbon leaders because of the clear water.

A Maligne Lake rainbow trout taken with a bead head nymph.

I should caution that there can be a silt load in parts of the lake during the June runoff. Longer (at least 12 feet) is better when it comes to leaders in the usually crystal clear waters of Maligne Lake. Colourful streamers are recommended by just about everybody who fly fishes Maligne Lake: Doc Spratley, Mickey Finn, Little Brook Trout and Little Rainbow Trout, along with Full Back Mayfly Nymphs and Double Shrimp. Hand tied streamer patterns with some sparkle are also a good bet.

Blind casts are generally a waste of time. Usually, you have to troll (fast), cover a lot of ground and hope to bump into some fish. Let out enough line to get down 10–15 feet (into the strike zone), and rip the line forward as often as possible. Although trolling is not the only way to catch trout in Maligne Lake, it's one of the better techniques. Troll, troll and troll some more as you search out trout in bays and shoals.

When you reach some promising bays and shoals, switch tactics by doing some still fishing with the usual bead head nymphs and chironomid patterns. I'd suggest still fishing with a 5- to 6-weight rod and a floating line with a long leader rigged with a strike indicator set for the approximate depth of the water. Start by stripping some line. Make a roll cast over the gunwale of the boat, make a back cast, then a straight-line cast towards your target. Use the water to load the rod and gain added distance if necessary. Let the fly bob in the waves. If there's a trout in the vicinity, it will strike the nymph or chironomid pattern.

Trout often have a spotty distribution in Maligne Lake. They tend to be concentrated in certain holding water, and your job is to seek out these honey holes. The locations tend to vary depending on the chironomid hatch. Chironomids have an affinity for mud bottoms and marl substrates. They hatch periodically throughout

Maligne Lake brook trout will attack streamers.

This fly fisher has hooked a fish!

the open-water season. Find a chironomid hatch, and that's where the resident trout will be feeding. If there's no obvious chironomid hatch, locate trout by trolling streamers, then switch to bead head nymphs or chironomids fished with a slip bobber to clean the table. It's that simple. Leave your dry flies at home; they're generally non-producers.

You can expect highly unpredictable weather throughout the open-water season on Maligne Lake and could experience rain, snow, sunshine, wind and/or calm conditions (all in one day), so come prepared for all of these possible scenarios. On a good day you'll have plenty of action, but be patient as you try your hand at catching the feisty brook trout and rainbows. They're not everywhere, but you'll be rewarded if you're persistent. You'll also be enthralled with the scenery and a day on the water fly fishing amid the ragged peaks of the Alberta Rockies.

If You Go

Fishing Regulations: A fishing permit is required to fish in Jasper National Park. Check the Parks Canada—Jasper National Park website for the current fishing regulations in Jasper.

Guided trips can be booked in Jasper. Boat rentals are available on Maligne Lake at the Curly Phillips Boat House; no gas-powered motorboats are permitted, although electric motors are allowed. Check out Travel Alberta for vacation guides and the Parks Canada—Jasper National Park and the Municipality of Jasper websites for information regarding campsites, accommodations and restaurants.

Fish Creek Provincial Park boat launch on the Bow River.

Alberta's Unpredictable Lower Bow River

The lower Bow River downstream of Calgary has long featured some of Alberta's best fishing for both rainbow and brown trout and is the destination of choice for the itinerant fly fisher, although floats are also popular downstream of Banff National Park and Canmore. The lower section of the Bow River also has a large population of mountain whitefish and even the occasional pike, but these are not targeted by fly fishers.

Public access to the Bow River downstream of Calgary is limited due to private land ownership. Key fishing access sites are located at Fish Creek Provincial Park on the southeast edge of Calgary upstream of Highway 22; Policeman Flats several miles downstream; MacKinnon Flats; and finally Carseland upstream of Highway 24. Most

float trips are customized depending on the interests of the anglers and typically involve rather long floats between the fishing access sites.

Guides will tell you that fishing can be good during all seasons on the Bow River, but in my experience, it's best during July and August. I tend to favour the month of July because it's at this time of year that the rainbows have returned to the Bow from spawning streams in the headwaters of the Highwood River—they're lean, hungry and on the feed.

Dry fly fishing on the Bow River is usually best during late summer, especially using hopper patterns up tight against the bank. Fishing with bead head nymphs and San Juan Worms can be dynamite at any time of year and is probably one of the most popular techniques during summer and autumn, while streamer fishing with Bow

River Buggers or a black Gartside leech is probably best during spring and early summer when flows are high.

Don Pike is the head guide of the Bow River Company, based in Calgary. He's been guiding on the river since 1975. Pike is one of the veterans, along with Barry White, who heads up the Bow River Anglers; they are the two guides I've spent most of my time with on this world-renowned trout stream, along with Aaron Caldwell of Fish Tales Fly Shop.

Even if you think you know all the answers, there will be days when fishing might be slow and you're going to be second guessing yourself. Streamer fishing on this regulated river is no slam dunk and is best done in a Mackenzie-style drift boat—most of the time you'll earn your fish, despite those days when fishing is red hot and you think you've died and gone to trout heaven.

Why can it be so difficult to predict what the fishing is going to be like on the Bow River, which is, after all, a tail-water stream rather than a typical freestone river? Being a tail-water stream, flows are relatively stable downstream of Bearspaw Reservoir,

Don Pike with a Bow River rainbow trout.

a TransAlta hydroelectric reservoir just upstream of metropolitan Calgary.

You have to hit the river at just the right time—when the water is running jade green, fast and high, and trout are pushed up against the stream banks—for the best action. This happens particularly at the tail end of the runoff. Some years, there may

The Bow River can be unpredictable, but always enjoyable.

Myles Radford with a Bow River brown trout.

morning, right up to closing time as the sun sets. I've had days when hook-ups were in the dozens. Even if you don't hit pay dirt, you should be able to catch at least a few trout in the 20-inch range.

The lower Bow River is loaded with fish. Biologists estimate there are about 1500 catchable-size trout—fish 10 inches or bigger—per mile in the 112-mile (180-kilometre) section downstream of Calgary to the Bassano Dam. A new-found bonus is that the size of the trout in the lower Bow just keeps going up since new, special regulations were established in 2001, with a minimum size and new catch limit. You rarely catch a small trout, less than 16–18 inches, when fishing with streamers. The small trout are typically taken when fly fishing with nymphs or dry flies. Bow River rainbows are more like a steelhead than a typical rainbow trout; they're sleek and are chrome bodied with brute strength. The browns are stocky, well-coloured behemoths—sturdy as a fence post.

I've had good success when fishing with a cone head Woolly Bugger (black and olive) and Marabou Leech (black or olive) on the Bow River. Pike has always been sold on the Bow River Bugger, with the Gartside Leech (black, olive or white) a close second; both of these patterns are usually well-stocked in Calgary fly shops. Pike tends to lean towards the Bow River Bugger—a cross between a Woolly Bugger and a Muddler Minnow—because it's easier to pick up with its white head when it's in the water. There are many variations of the Bow River Bugger, but the "original" pattern, with its white head, is an old standby. Barry White recommends Woolly Buggers, Muddler Minnows, Zonkers, Bow River Buggers and the Bunny Fly. These are just a few good search patterns to test the water. Most streamer hooks should be in the size 2–6 range, which tend to attract large trout. Barry White is fond of saying,

not be a well-defined runoff, or it may be short lived, both of which can have an impact on fishing success. It also doesn't hurt if the water level is stable (more or less) during your trip because trout can get shy as they try to find their comfort zone when levels fluctuate during transition flows. If spring runoff is low, all bets are off regarding where the trout might be found, and since the major 2013 flood, they've often been found in midstream buckets after the cutbanks were eroded.

I like streamer fishing on the lower Bow River best during in June and July because flows are usually most suitable during these months. While there are no guarantees, if you're patient and stick with some proven patterns, you'll likely be rewarded. Other times can also be productive for streamer fishing, however. One other suggestion: fish the whole day. I've caught trout—both browns and rainbows—just minutes after hitting the water early in the

A rainbow trout from the Bow River taken on a Marilyn Monroe fly pattern.

"Go big and ugly to catch big and ugly." "Big bite to get a big bite" is another phrase he uses.

Regarding your rod and line, I suggest using a minimum of a 6-weight rod, preferably 8-weight, with a matching, sinking tip line when fishing with streamers. Some guides recommend overloading the line weight—for example, using an 8-weight line on a 7-weight rod—to improve casting distance and ease of casting. Short leaders are the order of the day when fishing big, swift streams such as the lower Bow. Cut them down to no more than 3 feet (or even 18 inches) so streamers are in the strike zone almost as soon as they hit the water. You don't have to worry about lining trout when you're fishing streamers up tight against the river bank; a long leader is a handicap.

Make sure that your fly line is clean and lubricated with line dressing before heading out. You'll work hard when streamer fishing, and you want the least possible friction and line resistance when casting during the day. Because you'll be doing a lot of casting on this large river, casting options are important; as well as picking out the better lies, you need to keep looking out the corner of your eye to see what's coming up when fishing from a drift boat.

One of the most effective ways to fish the Bow with streamers is from a drift boat so you can stay within casting range of the banks. When flows are bank full, I use two basic types of casts when fishing streamers from a drift boat. First, cast downstream ahead of the drift boat, or at right angles to the bank. Follow through with two sharp upstream mends to help sink the fly line. Let the streamer come out toward the drift

Swim flies tight to the stream bank.

boat in a dead drift. Second, cast upstream behind the drift boat, or at right angles to the bank. Give the line a quick downstream mend. Swim the fly up tight against the bank in a dead drift until it swings towards the boat. During a dead drift, twitch the fly from time to time—once the drift ends, strip the line as you retrieve it. Don't waste your time and energy false casting. Pitch the streamer towards the bank after stripping adequate line, and leave the line in the water to load the rod on your next cast. There's nothing fancy about streamer fishing, but it is important to work the line to fish streamers effectively. It's a good technique because you're using large flies that attract large fish.

You have to develop an eye for trout lairs. While most trout will be near the bank, you should also fish seams between currents with different speeds, foam lines, "buckets" near underwater structures such as dead or woody debris and in front of and behind large boulders, edges of bars,

Mackenzie-style drift boats are the way to go on the Bow River.

Walk-and-wade fishing lets an angler take their time through prime holding water.

cut banks…any pockets where there's some slack water for a trout to hide and rest. When the water is fast and high, the trout will either be up tight against a stream bank, down low in typical pools or a quiet backwater, or side channels, all places where they can avoid strong currents and conserve their strength.

From time to time, you'll get out of a drift boat for some walk-and-wade fishing in prime holding water. You can fly fish in conventional ways (i.e., by casting upstream) with a streamer under these circumstances using basic straight-line casts and roll casts, depending on the conditions, and then fish with a dead drift. However, it's usually easier to fish a streamer when wading downstream.

Point the tip of your rod towards the fly whether you're in a drift boat or walk-and-wade fishing—keep the rod tip down low

in anticipation of a strike. Hook-ups will be more or less automatic after a trout strikes—big fish tend to hit like a sledge-hammer, and you usually don't have to worry about setting the hook. There is a tendency for hard-mouthed trout to throw a barbless hook, so make sure the tip is sharp at all times if you fish barbless hooks. Also, don't try to bring the fish to reel until you have it under control—that first few seconds after a hook-set is critical in landing trout, so play the fish with your hand on the line at the start until you have it under control.

Although some of the best times to fish with streamers in the Bow River are in June and July, you can catch big trout at any time of the year with streamers. Streamer fishing on the lower Bow River can be a bit of a crap shoot, but if you get it down right, it's about as good as it gets!

Southwestern Alberta Dream Float Trips

If You Go

Many fishing guides ply the Bow River. Search online for guides and contact information. Check out the Travel Alberta website's fishing link for further options.

Several Calgary fly shops provide guided float trips on the lower Bow River, including Barry White Bow River Anglers, Bow River Hookers, Bow River Troutfitters, Country Pleasures Flyfishing, Fish Tales Fly Shop & Guide Service and West Winds Fishing Guide Service.

Southwestern Alberta—long billed as the place where the prairies meet the mountains—features stunning vistas set against the backdrop of the jagged Alberta Rockies. An area that's home to some of Alberta's premier trout streams, featuring dream fly fishing float trips on the Castle, Oldman and Waterton rivers.

The Castle and Oldman rivers are legendary Alberta "blue ribbon" trout streams with native cutthroats and long-established rainbows, while the brown trout fishing on the Waterton River is a star on the rise. Mountain whitefish are plentiful in all of these rivers. Bull trout skulk in deep pools, still on the road to recovery since zero limits were imposed in 1995 after populations were judged fragile by government officials.

I've been on all these floats, and the Castle, Oldman and Waterton rivers have a long-standing tradition as fine fisheries in their own right.

Southwestern Alberta features several dream float trips.

A Castle River float trip is exciting and picturesque.

Castle River

The Castle River is arguably one of the most scenic floats in all of southern Alberta as it abruptly winds its way from the eastern slopes of the Alberta Rockies into the narrow band of foothills and eventually reaches the prairies through a varied and picturesque landscape.

Basically, there are two key float trips on this section of the river: (1) from the Castle Falls Campground in the Forest Reserve downstream of Highway 774 down to the Castle River Rodeo Grounds just downstream of Highway 507; and (2) from the Castle River Rodeo Grounds down to the bridge crossing on the old Highway 3 above the Oldman River Dam. There's a narrow window of opportunity to float these two sections of the Castle River, from the tail end of the runoff in mid-June until mid-July, after which the river is usually too shallow to float.

The upper float has its hairy moments because there are many white-water sections to navigate and some heart-stopping falls and cascades associated with sandstone chutes—it's not for the faint of heart. However, there's lot of fishable water, especially below the confluence of the Castle and Carbondale rivers.

The lower float is a gentleman's trip by comparison, but the stretch of river below Beaver Mines in Zoratti's Canyon is a rather exciting section that features lots of white water and terrific scenery with many outstanding pools. The views are so breathtaking in the bowels of Zoratti's Canyon that it's hard to focus on fishing.

Zorrati's Canyon is a highlight of the lower Castle float trip.

The Castle River is a fly fisher's delight and the only stream in Alberta where I've had a Grand Slam in one day fishing with dry flies—landing cutthroat trout, rainbow trout, bull trout and mountain whitefish all on the same trip in the upper section. The lower section features mainly rainbows up to about 16 inches in size, although there are some bull trout in the vicinity of its confluence with Mill Creek.

Local guides recommend using a hopper-dropper pattern that features an attractor fly such as a Madame X or a Turks Tarantula and a dropper bead head nymph tied off the eye of the fly or the shank of the attractor pattern to double your money during a float trip, or when walk-and-wade fishing on rivers such as the Castle and Oldman rivers in particular.

Oldman River

Float trips on the Oldman River are on a couple of sections above the Oldman River Dam located downstream of Highway 22: (1) from Highway 22 to a bridge crossing on a secondary road near Olin Creek; and (2) from the Olin Creek crossing to just above the Oldman River Dam. Below the dam, floats go downstream to the Summerview Bridge just above the Piikani Nation reserve. The sections above the dam are best fished between mid-June and mid-July, whereas below the dam, floats are possible (with rubber rafts) up until October most years because the flows are regulated in the tail water downstream of the dam.

Fly fishing on the Oldman River below the dam.

Above the Oldman River Dam, the Oldman River is a rather swift freestone river that has long runs interspersed with infrequent deep pools. Below the dam, it is rather tame by comparison. Both above and below the dam, the scenery is characterized by rolling ranch land and native prairies with stands of large cottonwoods in many areas. This is some of Alberta's best cattle country. The scenery below the Oldman River Dam is particularly outstanding and features many dramatic landscapes with rugged cliffs and placid pools and runs. There are lots of spots both above and below the dam where walk-and-wade fishing is a must-do, so expect frequent stops to test the water.

The river upstream of the dam features primarily rainbow trout, with some bull trout, lots of mountain whitefish and the occasional brown trout thrown into the mix below the Oldman River Dam. Most fly fishers target the rainbows using hopper-droppers or streamer patterns. It's probably a good idea for the sport up front on a float trip to use a hopper-dropper rig or large attractor pattern while the angler in the stern should fish with streamers, just to cover your bases.

Waterton River

The Waterton River features two key sections for float trips: (1) from just upstream of the Highway 6 bridge crossing in Waterton Lakes National Park to a bridge crossing on a secondary road a few miles east of Twin Butte; and (2) from the bridge crossing east of Twin Butte downstream to a bridge on a secondary road just below

The upper Oldman River is best fished in early summer.

the Palmer Ranch several miles east of Highway 6. The window for float trips on both of these sections is short, from mid-June until mid-July, after which it's a tough float in shallow water.

Both sections meander through the Alberta prairies, and you'd swear you were an early explorer, the area has changed so little over the past century since the land was initially homesteaded. This is in the heartland of Alberta's ranch lands, very pastoral and quiet—save for occasional shrieks of red-tailed hawks—with the smell of fresh-cut hay in the air during the summer months.

The Waterton River features excellent dry fly fishing for brown trout, in particular, in both sections, but also for rainbows, especially in the lower section. Hopper patterns are go-to flies—for example, the Mo Joe Hopper and the Frankenhopper Parachute—for both browns and rainbows, fished in promising lairs up close to the stream bank and along seams or under foam lines. While I haven't taken any large brown trout (yet) in the Waterton River, I've seen some dandies, and with any luck, one of these days I'll land a real lunker. You can expect to catch both brown and rainbow trout to about 16–18 inches, all day long.

The Waterton River is one of the few waters where you can realistically expect to take browns on a dry fly rather than a streamer, and you don't have to hunt them down like you would on the Red Deer River, for example. The rainbows are gravy on a float trip.

Gearing up inflatable raft for a float down the Waterton River.

Cree River Lodge, Saskatch-ewan: Northern Pike Capital of the World

Try a dry fly to catch brown trout on the Waterton River.

If you want to get off the beaten track away from the crowds, consider booking a float trip with one of the local fly shops or fishing guides in Bellevue or Coleman for a fly fishing adventure on the Castle, Oldman or Waterton rivers. You'll be treated to some of Alberta's best scenery and fly fishing, and once you're hooked there'll be no turning back. You'll be a full-fledged member of Alberta's fly fishing junkie community.

If You Go

The Crowsnest Angler fly shop in Bellevue and the Crowsnest Fly Shop and Café in Coleman provide guided float trips on the Castle, Oldman and Waterton rivers.

I've had the pleasure to fly fish for pike, Arctic grayling and walleye twice at the Cree River Lodge, the first time in 2008 with my son and the second time with my wife in 2012. I can hardy wait to go back again. It was pike fishing at its best! The lodge is situated on the Cree River a short distance from Wapata Lake, just south of Stony Rapids, a small settlement east of Lake Athabasca. Pat Babcock of White Fox, Saskatchewan, is currently the sole owner of the Cree River Lodge.

As with most trips to a fly-in fishing lodge in Saskatchewan, clients generally depart on Transwest Air from Saskatoon, the provincial northern transportation hub, much like Edmonton is the gateway to the north in Alberta. From Saskatoon, Transwest Air is the principle carrier that ferries clients to various lodges en route to Stony Rapids, itself another hub for various lodges in the vicinity. Our plane stopped at several airstrips where clients departed for various lodges before we arrived at Stony Rapids. Myles and I then took a 1954 de Havilland Beaver float plane from Stony Rapids to the Cree River Lodge. The ancient Beaver is truly the workhorse of bush planes in Canada's north, still reliable after all the years since the model was originally built.

The Cree River Lodge bills itself as the "Northern Pike Capital of the World." I'd say this is definitely an accurate assessment, based on my experience at various Canadian fish camps. Not only are there lots of pike, but you also really do have a legitimate shot at 40- to 50-inch pike on any given day. And that's fly fishing for pike, not using hardware. In my books, any pike over 36 inches is a fine trophy.

The Cree River Lodge is only accessible by float plane.

As a bonus, the area is lousy with walleye, and it also boasts excellent Arctic grayling fishing. Although both the Cree River and nearby Wapata Lake feature great walleye fishing, we were having so much fun catching monster pike and trophy Arctic grayling that we mostly gave the walleye a break.

The Cree River Lodge has long had a policy of catch-and-release fishing with barbless hooks only. It would be a shame to take any of the large pike, although some smaller pike and walleye are eaten for shore lunches. They're the only lodge on Wapata Lake and in fact the only lodge on the Cree River system between Cree Lake and Black Lake; consequently, they have little fishing pressure, which translates into good fishing year after year. You don't have to worry about being blown off the water during a trip to the Cree River Lodge. There's always an opportunity to enjoy some fishing close to camp regardless of the weather.

The lodge features cozy, modern cabins.

The lodge is open from June 1 to September 15, annually. It features five modern cabins with wood-burning stoves, separate bedrooms with comfortable beds, showers, indoor toilets, a sitting area and veranda. Clean linens and bedding are provided daily. The maximum capacity of the Cree River Lodge is 16 people; Pat will make special arrangement during July and August to accommodate parties with 12 or more people in a group for sessions such as conventions or team-building meetings.

Fresh coffee is delivered to your cabin at 6:00 AM. Breakfast is served in the main lodge at 7:00 AM. A shore lunch is prepared by your guide at noon. At 5:00 PM you'll return to the lodge for appetizers. A buffet style, all you can eat, evening meal is served in the main lodge at 6:00 PM. There's also a bar service, including wine. Arrangements can be made for some after-dinner fishing if you decide not to kick back after your day on the water.

I really appreciated the lodge's 16-foot Lund Alaskan boats, which have a spacious open floor design and swivel seats, as well as enclosed storage areas to keep items dry and secure. These boats are among the best I've ever seen for fly fishing in many trips to numerous fishing lodges across Canada. There was nothing to snag a fly line on, which made for worry-free casting for both sports in the boat.

The boats are powered by 40-horsepower, 4-stroke Yamaha outboards and are operated by experienced local Dene fishing guides who know the area like the back of their hands. During my first trip, my son and I were paired up with Joe Toutsaint from the nearby Black Lake First Nations settlement. He was a great guide, and I've never seen anyone fillet fish faster than Joe. A shore lunch is a tradition at a Canadian fishing lodge, and Joe and his partner, Louie John Martin, cooked up a dandy for

A typical shore lunch of fresh pike and walleye fillets with fried potatoes.

us on the first day of our trip. Despite having a rather late start on day one of our arrival, I got off to a good start with my largest northern pike taping 37 inches, and my son, Myles, besting me with a 44-inch brute—all on a fly rod. It got better, though. On my last day, once I found the groove, I landed a 41-inch beauty and two 44-inch monsters. Plus, Myles tied the score with another 44-inch behemoth of his own—not bad for a short trip. Fly fishing for pike just doesn't get any better than that. I actually lost count of how many pike I landed that ranged from 36 to 40 inches on my best day; there were so many I didn't even break out the camera unless they topped 40 inches, the fishing was that good.

The author with lodge owner Pat Babcock, holding a trophy pike.

We had timed our late June trip perfectly. Slender shoots of equisetum were just emerging in the shallow bays, and water lilies were starting to bud out—submergent aquatic plants were but a faint promise in the shallows. Winds were generally calm. Daytime temperatures ranged from 20 to 25° C. Water temperature held steady at about 15° C, which is just about perfect for pike fishing. And they were hungry—it shaped up as the perfect storm for pike fly fishing.

An additional feature at the lodge is an exciting side-trip to vast sand dunes south of the lodge along the tortuous Cree River,

This pike was released to swim another day.

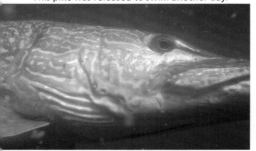

which I highly recommend. The scenery along the Cree River is spectacular, featuring pristine boreal forest and riparian areas. Not only are the sand dunes a sight to behold, but there's also fantastic fishing along the route, with many outstanding pike in the 40-inch–plus range. At "Noname" lake near the sand dunes, Myles and I caught three pike that topped 44 inches, all on fly rods, while another member of our party took one that reached 47 inches using spinning gear.

I guess that the only downside of a fly-in fishing trip to the Cree River Lodge is that once it's over, everything else seems so very inconsequential, leaving you with that melancholy feeling in the pit of your stomach. Think Saskatchewan if big pike are on your bucket list, and mark the Cree River Lodge as a must-fish destination.

If You Go

For reservations and information, contact the Cree River Lodge by visiting their website.

A Lesson from the Grand River, Ontario

Outdoorsmen can take a page from the volunteer work of the Friends of the Grand River in Ontario: a lesson on how to care for a river rendered incapable of supporting trout in the 1950s, that was rejuvenated and brought back to life in the 1990s as a result of habitat enhancement activities and brown trout stocking programs undertaken by local conservation groups and government agencies.

The Friends of the Grand River has been the lead organization behind the recovery program. The not-for-profit organization was established in 1995 in the town of Fergus to promote and implement projects to preserve and enhance the ecology of the Grand River watershed. It was spawned from what was once the Grand River chapter of Trout Unlimited Canada that

Volunteers have been key to the success of the Grand River recovery program (above and below).

A Grand River brown trout.

broke away after feeling disenfranchised from the parent body, frustrated that locally raised funds were being spent elsewhere in Canada.

The Grand River is a tail-water fishery downstream of Lake Belwood, a water storage reservoir, in the picturesque countryside north of Kitchener. It's largely a put-and-take brown trout fishery, although some spawning activity occurs, and there appears to be at least some natural reproduction. Its flows are similar in nature to many tail water fisheries in Alberta in places below reservoirs such as the Dickson Dam on the Red Deer River. There's a zero limit on trout, and no bait fishing is allowed; fishing is permitted only with artificial lures and single, barbless hooks. Compared with Alberta's trout streams, I'd categorize the Grand River as a technical stream where a large fly would be size 20 on downwards. It's relatively small by western standards, without a swift current,

and it can be readily fished by walking and wading, although studded wading boots are recommended.

Members of the Friends of the Grand River hope that one day a self-sustaining fishery may eventually populate the Grand River. Although self-sustaining brown trout fisheries are notoriously difficult to kick-start and often take a decade or two to get going, that day may not be far off, having been an ongoing project since the 1990s.

Today, the Grand River has a reputation for growing large trout and is now a major tourist attraction for fly fishers throughout eastern Canada and the United States—thanks to the Friends of the Grand River. I met anglers from Montreal, Illinois and Colorado while on the water. The economic benefits have been positive for the local communities of Fergus and Elora. These towns reminded me of Ennis, Montana, a hotbed for fly fishing junkies in the west, and Fernie, BC.

I didn't see a single cow in the riparian zone along literally miles of river frontage during my trip, despite intensive dairy farming in the watershed. Larry McGratton, a member of the Friends of the Grand River, said this wasn't always the case, and stream bank damage was fairly common before the organization started working with farmers to curtail this problem. Volunteers from the Friends of the Grand River talked with local farmers and persuaded them to graze their cattle away from the river.

There was a time not so long ago that the Grand River was an open sewer—despoiled—with little in its polluted waters but coarse fish, carp and suckers, of no significant value for fishing. Farming and urbanization had warmed and silted the river, making it unsuitable for native brook trout and introduced brown trout during the first half of the 20th century.

Along came the Friends of the Grand River, a group of several hundred local volunteers whose goal was to clean up the polluted water and establish a trout fishery. Over the past couple of decades, this organization has partnered with like-minded conservation groups such as the Isaak Walton Fly Fishing Club, Trout Unlimited Canada, the Kitchener Waterloo Fly Fishers and Hamilton Fly Fishers and a host of other local organizations to work with the local Grand River Conservation Authority and area municipalities to improve water quality in the Grand River. They've picked up litter and planted willow shoots in unstable stream banks to provide some bank armour where erosion is a concern. They've worked to undertake fisheries research and fish enhancement projects, assisted with fish stocking, helped to raise awareness of the tourism benefits of fishing the Grand River through a Grand River Fly Fishing Forum and began a River Watch program to curtail poaching.

A River Watch program was begun to curtail poaching (above); volunteers planted willow shoots to prevent bank erosion (below).

The Friends of the Grand River also provides funds to secure easements for public access along the river; they've developed several parking areas in cooperation with municipal governments complete with garbage bins and access trails to the river. Some sites even include metal steps where a pitched grade leads to the river. I visited one access site in the town of Fergus that had a trail through a woman's flower garden, fashioned out of stepping stones. It can be done. Public access is a potentially controversial issue, so the organization goes out of its way to cooperate with local landowners to ensure they're onside and everything is hunky-dory.

Volunteers work with the Ontario Ministry of Natural Resources to stock brown trout annually, using pails when necessary to spread them around and ensure they're well distributed in the best quality water; otherwise, there's a good chance the hatchery officials would simply dump the trout in the river at bridge crossings and let nature take its course. Because the Grand River is a no-kill fishery, the Friends of the Grand River provides an alternate site where local children can catch trout they purchase through their fundraising programs. And they've worked with Ontario Hydro to install nesting platforms for osprey where once there were none, to provide bird-watching opportunities; the ospreys have taken to the area, much to the delight of bird watchers.

And that's not all. During the annual Friends of the Grand River hands-on Fly Fishing Forum, volunteers provide free fly fishing seminars, free fly casting lessons and a women's fly fishing course. They also provide used fly fishing equipment for sale, all in support of the Grand River conservation projects. Proceeds from this event go towards habitat and access improvement on the Grand River.

Volunteers work to stock the river annually.

Local children can fish at their own fishing pond.

The work of the Friends of the Grand River is paying dividends. In 2006, the organization, working in conjunction with some local partners, hosted the 4th annual Canadian National Fly Fishing Championships and Conservation Symposium on the Grand River and the nearby Conestogo River tail waters. These events raised over $7000 for future conservation programs and signalled to the rest of Canada the beneficial results of volunteer efforts and community involvement on the Grand River. The Friends of the Grand River is still going strong, and its website features details on the group's goals and activities.

Trout fishermen can take a page from the Friends of the Grand River on how to restore a trout stream, and perhaps none too soon on some of their local waters. Those volunteers made the Grand River a better trout stream for fly fishers from all over the world.

If You Go

Fergus and Elora are located in the epicentre of fly fishing opportunities on the Grand River. They're quintessential small Ontario towns with many charming accommodations and restaurants. Local businesses go out of their way to cater to fly angling enthusiasts. Check out their Grand & Gorgeous website online.

John Huff with a Lac Collins brook trout.

Fly Fishing on the Kenauk Reserve at Montebello, Quebec

It was billed as "an easy drive to another world" in a brochure for the Fairmont Kenauk private reserve at Montebello, Quebec. And as yet another brook trout lashed out at one of many hot flies of the day on Lac Collins, I couldn't help but agree. The trip had gotten off to a good start. I had a hook-up on my first cast. While the action wasn't exactly non-stop during the rest of the day, rare was the hour when my son, Myles, and I didn't

have a few brook trout on the line. As my wife, Adrienne, and I reflected on the day's events over dinner in the Chalet Muskrat, Myles was back on the lake for another go at the feisty brook trout.

It was more of the same on day two. We had the lake to ourselves, save for the services of our fishing guide, John Huff. Huff operates the Fly Fishing Guide Service for Kenauk and hosts trout fishing trips primarily out of two four-star chalets—Chalet Muskrat (brook trout on Lac Collins) and Chalet Pumpkinseed (rainbow trout on Pumpkinseed Lake)—in the reserve. He can also provide some unique fishing opportunities for rainbow trout and brown trout, as well as smallmouth bass fishing, on the Kinonge River. Huff is a noted Canadian fishing guide, and three-time captain and eight-time team member of the Canadian Fly Fishing Team, so being able to spend some time under his wing was a decided attraction. Fishing packages, summer adventures and autumn getaway trips can be booked without a guide, but I didn't want to take any chances, being unfamiliar with Kenauk, which has exclusive fishing rights on its managed waters.

Fishing pressure is tightly regulated in some Canadian provinces in what are termed "managed" waters. In New Brunswick they're called "Crown Reserve waters," where use is managed by a lottery. In Quebec they go by the names of "wildlife reserves" or a "ZEC" (a French acronym for "controlled harvesting zone"). Quebec also has some rivers where certain outfitting operations have exclusive rights. In British Columbia there are "classified waters." These provinces have taken steps to regulate public use on some of their water bodies, often those of the best quality that are highly productive. Lakes and streams in these managed waters have premium fishing opportunities for Atlantic salmon, steelhead, brook trout, pike and walleye.

In Quebec, to fish in wildlife reserves, you generally must make a reservation. You must also acquire a right of access or an authorization to fish, as the case may be, and comply with the date, time and location specified. When you are done fishing or at the end of your stay, you must report all fish caught. Furthermore, you must hold a right of access or an authorization to fish even to carry fishing tackle with you in these locations. Getaway packages are available at Quebec's wildlife reserves, such as a Family Fishing Package, which includes accommodations, a boat and a fishing pass for several lakes and rivers.

A ZEC is a fishing territory whose management has been delegated to a non-profit organization. To fish in a ZEC you must register and comply with the date, time and locations or sector specified on the proof of registration. This proof of registration must be carried and shown upon request to wildlife protection officers. The registration must be returned when the stay is over, and all catches must be declared to the body responsible for managing the ZEC in question.

Kenauk is one of the largest private nature reserves in North America. It's situated on land granted to the first bishop of Quebec by the King of France in 1674 north of the Ottawa River. The Seigniory Club, as it was previously known, became a favourite retreat for heads of state, royalty and celebrities. Kenauk consists of about 260 square kilometres (100 square miles) of fairly pristine wilderness—albeit there is some logging activity—in the boreal forest. Huff claims there are about 30 fishable lakes at Kenauk (out of 70 overall) with large and smallmouth bass, northern pike, and rainbow, eastern brook, brown and lake trout.

Taunton Lake, just one of the Kenauk reserve's many pristine lakes.

Myles Radford landing a brook trout at Lac Collins.

I'd never fished at an exclusive reserve before my trip to Kenauk and wasn't quite sure what to expect, considering that Kenauk is in a region of Canada that has long been settled. The main attraction was to catch some brook trout and go fishing on a lake that I would have to myself—no rubbing elbows with other fishermen this time. Access to the Kenauk reserve is gated, so you don't have to worry about anyone crashing your party. Secondly, my family would be staying in a four-star cabin—the Chalet Muskrat—a short hike from Lac Collins in a wilderness setting. Last, but not least, I'd have an opportunity to go fishing with John Huff, a fly fishing pro from eastern Canada, far from my home in Alberta, making this a unique experience.

I found the resonating call of bull frogs at night a bit odd and quite humourous, but those are about the only sounds you're likely to hear—the silence would be deafening if not for the bellowing of the bull

frogs. There's also an abundance of bird-life—flycatchers, great blue herons, common loons—and vivid purple lady's slipper abounds, depending on the season. Don't be surprised to see the odd white-tailed deer along the trails, or moose or beavers near water.

I did most of my fishing from the comfort of a boat, carefully standing at the bow, casting strategically and being careful not to hook the guide—a cardinal sin. For an added dimension to his fishing experience, Myles brought along a belly boat and enjoyed success fishing from it, as well as from the car top boat. It's easier for just one person to fly fish out of a car top boat if a guide is manning the oars, so Myles and I switched stations during the trip. When I wasn't in the boat I was on shore stretching my legs and still catching fish. We spelled off Huff from time to time so he could enjoy some fly fishing after rowing us all over the lake. We did precious little trolling, although we did catch a few fish using this technique. Most brook trout were in the 14- to 15-inch range, although one hit 18 inches—not bad for a lake in settled Canada.

Use a 4- to 5-weight rod and take both a floating and sink tip line (if you fish during the heat of summer, add a fast sinking line to get down into the strike zone, if necessary); 9-foot leaders will be okay. We fished with a wide selection of both dries, wet flies and streamers, as much to see what worked as what didn't. For more on brook trout techniques, see page 78.

The season starts at the end of April for trout; this is usually shortly after ice-out. It then continues past the normal closure of trout—at the end of September—into November. This extension is because Kenauk supports its fish stocks from its own hatchery. According to Huff, fall fishing for rainbows is great.

Bass fishing starts at the end of June. Bass are present in the Kinonge River throughout the season. Bass are also taken in Papineau, Whitefish and Maholey lakes (catch and release in Maholey). The latter two lakes also have pike. The best trout fishing in the Kinonge River is from mid-May to mid-June, although it can continue later if the river level stays up. Huff said that fishing is very good at Kenauk until it gets hot and dry in August. He always looks forward to autumn, when the cooling temperatures bring the fish back on top and puts them on the feed.

The Hornberg Special, along with (from left to right) the Egg Sucking Leech, San Juan Worm and Woolly Bugger.

A brook trout from Lac Collins.

My wife and I enjoyed our first trip to Kenauk so much that a few years later we made a repeat visit as a getaway vacation in autumn, to enjoy the splendour of the fall colours in eastern Canada as well as to spend some quiet time to get rejuvenated. Shopping for groceries in Quebec was an added bonus. The grocery stores have everything you need in the line of culinary delights for a few days in the outdoors—including fine wine. I'd say that the Kenauk brochure is on the mark with its claim that

"you can enjoy your privacy as well as some of the best fishing in Quebec." It's quiet, peaceful, and there is just so much solitude—these are the hallmarks of a stay in one of the backcountry cabins in Kenauk.

The Kenauk Reserve is located north of Montebello—there are 13 cabins to choose from on the reserve. The Chalet Muskrat has four bedrooms with double and single beds along with a Davenport. A couple of

Chalet Muskrat, Kenauk.

aluminum car top boats are at Lac Collins, along with oars. Most cabins feature fireplaces, and all have propane stoves, refrigerators, screened-in porches, indoor toilets, showers, private docks and boats, barbecues and fire pits. The kitchen and linen closet are both fully equipped. Bring your own food and beverages. There are no phones, faxes or television sets—or outlets for hair dryers—so you can leave your troubles behind. Your stay at the Kenauk reserve entitles you to full use of sports facilities at Le Chateau Montebello, Fairmont's four-star hotel next to the reserve.

If You Go

Fairmont Kenauk—the Seigniory at Montebello—is located on Highway 148, 110 kilometres east of Ottawa, Ontario. The property is protected by an agreement with the Société de la faune et des parcs du Quebec under article 36 (LRQ C-61.1) Contact the resort to make reservations.

New Brunswick's Miramichi River: Atlantic Salmon Showdown

Many anglers would say that Atlantic salmon, often called the King's fish, are the world's top freshwater game fish, and they could be correct. It was one of the most exciting moments of my life—a large Atlantic salmon on the end of my line made yet another run amid several leapers, stripping line well down to the backing as it ploughed downstream. The leapers were unnerving. These were not your smaller grilse, but large adults in the 10- to 20-pound range that exploded from the pool, becoming completely airborne before loudly splashing back into the water. One large salmon after another rocketed from the water as the tug of war raged on, scant yards from my station near the river's bank. I was a bundle of nerves. My heart was thumping. Yes, the leaper had indeed returned to the Miramichi River, New Brunswick—what a spectacle! I was having a great time, trying to even the score with my wife, Adrienne, who had landed a 16-pound salmon her first morning fishing. Talk about pressure!

Fishing guide Don Beek with Adrienne Radford after landing her Atlantic salmon.

"Every day is a little different," chimed Donald (Don) Beek, our guide, who resided in McNamee, New Brunswick. "You never know what they're going to hit." Actually, I don't understand why they'd take a fly in the first place because they're not supposed to feed in autumn as they prepare to spawn. Go figure.

"Cast at a 45-degree angle downstream, and let the fly drift out of the current. Do this two or three times, take a step downstream, and do it all over again," Don coached. "The salmon will hook itself, more or less. You don't want any slack line, so don't give it an upstream mend." That's all there is to it: a lot of straight-line casting for seven hours a day with maybe a hook-up or two as your reward—or, maybe no hook-ups at all. "The fish are playing hard to get," Don chuckled as I tied on yet another fly.

Catching an Atlantic salmon is near the pinnacle of success for fly anglers, and my dream had already come true at Pond's

Resort on the Miramichi River in New Brunswick, as the lip-hooked salmon continued to dog the line. The Miramichi is the stuff of legends, revered among fly fishers along with other famed Canadian Atlantic salmon streams such as the Cascapedia in Quebec's Gaspé Peninsula, Nova Scotia's Margaree, New Brunswick's renowned Restigouche, and perhaps the greatest of them all, Newfoundland's Humber River.

Despite the notoriety of all the great Atlantic salmon rivers in Canada, however, fly fishers routinely get skunked, often measuring their success by recalling swirls, or what they think might have been rises, near their flies during a week of hard fishing, seven-plus hours a day. That's what makes fly fishing for Atlantic salmon all the more interesting and rewarding when you finally catch one. There may be hundreds of fish in a pool, and none of them will strike.

The Miramichi River is famous for its Atlantic salmon.

Pond's Resort is a great place to stay for a fishing trip on the Miramichi.

My wife and I were bunked in a rustic cabin at Pond's Resort, a cluster of log cabins along with a dining room and guide shop nestled beside the fabled Miramichi River. The resort has been in business since the 1920s. It is located near Ludlow, about an hour's drive from Fredericton, the capital city of New Brunswick. Pond's has riparian rights to 16 salmon pools and 11 kilometres (7 miles) of river.

Speaking of riparian rights, I contacted Peter Cronin, then Director, Fisheries Branch, for clarification on access to angling waters in New Brunswick. Cronin said that the provincial government has a mandate of managing its natural resources in the best interest of the citizens of the province (including, but not exclusively for, anglers). Five water types generally describe angler access to New Brunswick waterways.

Water Class	%	Description
Private (Riparian)	43	Through the fundamental concept of property rights, a person may possibly own exclusive rights to fishing
Crown Open	33	Rivers or stretches of river open to angling to those in possession of a valid angling licence
Crown Reserve	12	Limited entry fishery, providing angling opportunity to residents of the province on a rod-per-day allocation
Crown Angling Leases	6	Public fisheries leased to private individuals, clubs or companies
Crown Closed	6	Waters closed to any type harvest for ~50 years or more (spawning sanctuaries)

Cronin advised that the level of public support for angling leases varies depending upon the individual interests in salmon or trout fishing. However, citizens of New Brunswick have broad support for the program, and this support is based essentially on the rent accrued, jobs created, economic benefits to local rural communities and the additional conservation or protection measures required by the lessees. He added, history on both sides of the Atlantic Ocean confirms that strong property rights provide fisheries owners with increased incentives to reduce fishing pressures, implement conservation measures and enhance stocks and their habitats. Knowing that they will gain from any activities that enhance their stocks, these individuals are more likely to engage in ecologically beneficial activities.

In New Brunswick, non-residents must fish in the company of a guide when angling for Atlantic salmon, as is the case for non-residents fishing in Newfoundland and Labrador. The guide is expected to keep the client on the right side of law, in addition to coaching him on how to try to catch one of these "fish of a thousand casts."

Atlantic salmon guides on the Miramichi River recommend using an 8-weight fly rod and floating line with an assortment of flies—Alley Shrimp, Green Machine and various Bomber patterns, in particular. Don Beek suggested the following wet fly patterns: Blue Charm, Green Machine, Blue Bomber and Mickey Finn. When I asked him why guides didn't recommend a sink tip line, he simply said that a floating line paid better dividends in his experience.

Non-residents must fish in the company of a guide.

Just to show that it really can be done, Adrienne hooked a large Atlantic salmon in the first pool we fished on the first morning of our trip—it was a 16-pound (at least) beauty—and she landed it at 10:30 AM. I'd earlier landed a grilse to get on the board and closed the day with a 12-pound salmon at about 4:00 PM on an Alley Shrimp. For the most part, we flogged an old Atlantic salmon guide fly: the Green Machine with orange on top and white on the bottom. Day one had exceeded our expectations.

A selection of Atlantic salmon flies.

We were back at it again the next morning by 9:30 AM, which turned out to be a slow day with only one grilse caught by another member of our party, from New York State, just before lunch. Despite the slow bite, it was one of those life moment events—just fishing the storied Miramichi River, listening to Beek's advice, taking in the grandeur of the autumn scenery as the river slipped quietly by.

This Atlantic salmon grilse will eventually grow much larger.

The legendary Miramichi River did not disappoint.

Towards evening we were fishing a pool by Nelson Hollow Bridge downstream of Pond's that was just packed with big salmon—they were everywhere, leaping and splashing about, causing a big commotion. My nerves were a bit jangled as I tied on a hand-tied bitch fly courtesy of Don. It wasn't long before I had a strike; that's when the leapers shifted into high gear, and my nerves really began to get frazzled. After the salmon was finally tailed and gently released, I laid down my rod; it was a perfect moment that wouldn't get any better, and I was content to call it a day.

My old buddy Perry Munro, Nova Scotia Master Guide for over 30 years who was fishing out of Pond's Resort during my stay, philosophized, "Duane, [usually] in a couple of days you might, and I mean might, have one [Atlantic salmon] on maybe. The group that was there before us guided by Bill [Ensor] and Don got three fish in four days. A series of circumstances led, I feel, to our success. Low water in the river stacked the fish in the pools that Pond's had rights to. The water was warm before we came, but a couple cold nights brought the water temperature down and made the fish active just when we came. We lucked out, and good on us!"

If You Go

Pond's Resort on the Miramichi is a quaint, Orvis-endorsed lodge on the banks of the Miramichi River, near Porter Cove, New Brunswick, that features fly fishing for Atlantic salmon in exclusive pools. Look them up online.

Newfoundland's Tuckamore Lodge

Tuckamore Lodge is an Orvis-endorsed lodge that's located a stone's throw from Main Brook on the Northern Peninsula of Newfoundland. The word "tuckamore" is a Newfie term for gnarled and tangled stands of stunted spruce and balsam fir trees. Such forests are characteristic of the Northern Peninsula, which is subject to rather harsh weather. This area is wind-swept, so be prepared for tough fly casting; you'll have to lean into your cast and lower your trajectory at times. According to the Tuckamore Lodge website, "Guests at Tuckamore Lodge have the opportunity to put their angling skills to the test while they cast a line for Atlantic salmon, the king of sport fish." There are no guarantees that you'll catch any Atlantic salmon, which have a reputation for being a rather challenging quarry. Flow conditions, water temperatures, the nature of the run and fishing pressure all impact angling success.

The runs of fresh salmon are also not entirely predictable, although large fish generally enter freshwater brooks first, followed by smaller adults. Local lore suggests that runs tend to peak when there's a full moon, which is associated with high tides that bring salmon into local streams. According to most experts, adult salmon do not feed while in fresh water; their stomachs are devoid of food, which makes catching them tricky if they're off the feed. Don MacLean, former Nova Scotia Fisheries Branch Director (now retired) and a licenced Newfoundland fishing guide, said, "Atlantic salmon remain a mystery to me, but I think there is enough evidence that they will at least pick stuff off the surface. I have also read of finding them with gravel in their stomach." Unlike Pacific salmon, adults don't die after they spawn; rather they return to the ocean.

The Northern Peninsula is peppered with many fine Atlantic salmon brooks.

The author makes a cast for Atlantic salmon in Newfoundland.

While the Tuckamore Lodge website claims that their Atlantic salmon "weigh an average of six to ten pounds," I personally didn't see any in that size range during my trip; most were much smaller, even though the timing was such that there should have been some large salmon in the local brooks (in Newfoundland, streams are called "brooks" and lakes are called "ponds").

If salmon are around you'll see them, especially fresh fish, which are silver and not hard to spot even in the tea-coloured water in local brooks. Plus, Atlantic salmon frequently leap out of the water, which is a dead giveaway they're present. Their scientific name is *Salmo salar*, with *salar* meaning "leaper." It is not known why Atlantic salmon leap out of the water, but they do it all the time, especially when congregated in schools. At times there's sheer pandemonium with leaping salmon, which can be rather unnerving to say the least.

The fishing season for Atlantic salmon in Newfoundland runs from June to September, and during this time the weather on the Northern Peninsula can range from being rather warm to outright chilly. During my trip in late June–early July, ambient temperatures were 7–25° C, all in the same week. My wife, Adrienne, and I fished several different brooks (e.g., Beaver Brook, Fisheries River, Main River, Salmon River, etc.) out of the lodge, whose water temperatures ranged from 15 to 16° C during our stay. According to *Soucie's Field Guide of Fishing Facts* (1988), the preferred water temperature of Atlantic salmon ranges from 10 to 17° C, so unfavourable water temperatures were no excuse for not catching a lot of salmon—actually, water temperatures were ideal.

Northern Peninsula brooks can be treacherous to navigate by foot; use caution.

The fly fishing drill for Atlantic salmon in Newfoundland calls for casting across and down a brook, generally using an 8-weight rod rigged with a floating line and a tapered leader, high sticking a wet fly when necessary and/or letting a dry fly (such as a bomber) float in a dead drift. When fishing in brooks, casting both upstream and downstream, mending is necessary to ensure a drag-free drift depending on the nature of the current. It isn't necessary to high stick the fly to the degree necessary in swift-flowing free-stone rivers in western Canada. Rather, hold your fly rod at about a 45-degree angle during the drift and simply let a wet fly swing in the current. The brooks near the lodge are relatively slow moving, so a weighted wet fly isn't necessary.

A word of caution regarding the substrate in brooks in Newfoundland: they have an irregular-sized cobble substrate that features smooth Precambrian rock of various sizes. The cobble can be treacherous to navigate, particularly because of the tea-coloured water drained from bogs. Be certain to wear polarized sunglasses to reduce

the glare and as an aid to seeing the bottom. Take one careful step at a time, feeling for solid footholds as you ford a brook. If you're mobility challenged, I highly recommend carrying a wading staff. Simms and Orvis carry top-line collapsible wading staffs.

While we went though our fly boxes searching for a hot fly, none of the patterns were producers even though most of the ones I used were hand tied by a veteran Newfoundland guide who's an old friend of mine. I fished with all the usual suspects: Blue Charms, Bombers, Green Machines and several variations of

Some Atlantic salmon flies.

Adrienne Radford tries her hand fly fishing for Atlantic salmon in Newfoundland.

Thunder and Lightning and White Wulff patterns, plus many, many bitch flies. I think a Blue Charm or Green Machine would be the choice patterns, however.

I was rather surprised at just how popular Atlantic salmon fishing is with the locals on the Northern Peninsula. There were lots of resident anglers out chasing salmon just about everywhere we ventured. For non-residents, there are some unique fishing regulations that apply. For example, a non-resident of the province cannot angle for any species of fish in any inland waters in Newfoundland and Labrador without engaging the services of an outfitter. The Newfoundland and Labrador Outfitters Association does not maintain a public list of licenced fishing guides. Consequently, non-residents are generally required to enlist the services of an outfitter to engage a licenced guide. Artificial flies must be

used for salmon and trout angling on scheduled salmon waters. Regulations describe an artificial fly as a single barbless hook dressed with materials to attract fish, so be sure to bring pliers to pinch down the barbs on barbed fly hooks.

According to the provincial angling regulations, anglers fishing in Newfoundland and Labrador are not permitted to catch and retain any salmon where the salmon measures 63 cm (24.8 inches) or greater. In other words, the salmon must be less than 63 cm long; a measuring tape should be part of your gear. According to Sam Whiffen of Fisheries and Oceans Canada, Newfoundland and Labrador, this measurement is always "fork length" in a species with a forked tail, not "total length" when the tail is pinched. By definition, Whiffen says length means, in respect to a fish, the distance measured in a straight line from the tip of its nose to the centre of the fork of its tail or, where there is no fork, to the tip of its tail. A salmon tag licence must be immediately affixed through the gills and mouth of kept fish, and the month and date must be cut out of the paper tag. A knife or scissors are necessary for this purpose. Make certain you cut out the correct date and month to stay within the law, or you'll run the risk of being charged and losing your catch and fishing poles.

The lodge has fine accommodations, and the food is good. Wildflowers were in bloom as well as the Labrador tea, and we especially delighted in the profusion of marsh marigolds. We saw lots of wildlife: woodland caribou, several of Newfoundland's ubiquitous moose, mink, snowshoe hares, robins, songbirds and spruce grouse. I have never in my life seen so many black flies, no-see-ums and mosquitoes, possibly because there was so much snowfall the previous winter. They were like a plague! Be sure to pack insect repellent and

perhaps a head net if flies bother you. Some antiseptic ointment would also be a good idea to deal with black fly bites.

The billing on a Tuckamore Lodge brochure pretty well summed things up: "There are really no guarantees in the outfitting business, except that we will do everything in our power to see that you have the best wilderness adventure imaginable. We want you to come back."

If You Go

Tuckamore Lodge is located 2.2 kilometres from the village of Main Brook and a 20-minute drive from the local airport at St. Anthony. Non-resident anglers would normally fly into either Deer Lake or St. Anthony and be picked up by lodge staff. Check out their website online.

Tuckamore Lodge is located near Main Brook on the Northern Peninsula.

The author with an eastern brook trout, Awesome Lake Lodge, Labrador.

Labrador's Awesome Lake Lodge

Don't get me wrong, I'm not bragging, but I broke what was then the New York state record for brook trout three times (all over 5 pounds) in one week at Awesome Lake Lodge in the Labrador wilderness, thanks to my fishing guide, Orville Caddy—no small feat considering what we were up against. Fishing was that good!

Alexis Thuillier, who used to guide out of Painter's Lodge in Campbell River, British Columbia, once lamented, "You can go from a hero to a zero in four hours!" So goes the saying among west coast fishing guides. If the fishing is good during a four-hour shift, the clients are happy campers, but if they get skunked, the guide pays the price. When on the water, a guide had better be able to carry the conversation, keep a client engaged and then pray for some

hook-ups. And when you're on an extended trip at a remote lodge and the fishing is slow, the challenge is even greater, as I found out at Awesome Lake—particularly when the weather is foul and you're on the water all day long, being buffeted by wind and rain.

I've been on guided fishing trips all across Canada and found the Labrador guides are in a class of their own. They're colourful characters, salt-of-the-earth outdoor folks who hunt, trap and fish. They're amiable and unpretentious. They're fun loving; they sing and dance and tell great jokes. They are honest and hard working. They're patient, obliging and quiet spoken.

Orville Caddy didn't pull any punches upon my arrival at the remote Awesome Lake Lodge. Head guide at the lodge, he wasted no time calling a huddle of the newly arrived sports as soon as their bags had been stored after disembarking from the Tamalik Air Twin Otter. "Boys," he said, "I've got to be up front with you all: the fishin's been slow for the past two weeks. Real slow. We've had rain, winds so hard we've been blown off the water. The sports have pounded the river and lined every trout dozens of times, to make it even worse. It's been tough fishing, I tell you."

It was a sobering introduction. The new sports had that worried look—one of shattered dreams. Small wonder the stone-faced party waiting to leave didn't have big smiles as they watched us arrive. The other guides—Jim Martin, Craig Blake and Hebert White—had their heads down. And so the week-long adventure began. Although it was not on a high note, at least we knew what we were up against.

I was the only Canadian in a party of seven sports during my trip to Awesome Lake, featuring fly fishing only. The other clients were from Maine and New York. They were serious fishermen, come to fly fish for big brook trout. After all, we were in the wilds of Labrador, and nothing short of trophy-sized trout would do—lots of them, hopefully.

The guides' friendly banter and entertainment made up for any lack of action on the water: Hebert, with his unexpected wild goose calls; Jim, with his singing and dancing; Orville and Craig, with tales of caribou hunts and living off the land; Jim's stories of plane crashes, a firsthand encounter with Bigfoot, locally known as the "Hairy Man," sightings of which date back almost 100 years in Labrador annals; Orville's use of caribou hair for hand tying flies and crafting popular local patterns such as mice and lemmings. The guides told us how they helped build and remodel the lodge at Awesome Lake and regaled us with stories about the sturdy Gander River boats, including how the guides ferried these sleek craft into Awesome Lake. We heard about the legends behind the named

Fly fishing at the mouth of the English River, Labrador.

pools on the English River, the outlet stream from Awesome Lake: Parker Pool, Lennie's Run, Rich's Run, Penny Falls, East-man's Edge, Trout Bite Finger, Thunder-dome, Beyond Thunderdome, Monster Alley, Caribou Island, Gloria's Hole, Mid-way, Double Honey Hole, Hell Hole, Peter's Pleasure, The Retreat, 6 Mile Flat…

The Labrador fishing guides made the day. I went to bed at night thinking about Hairy Men, plane crashes in the wilderness, caribou hunts and wilderness lore. "The biggest thing is, you know, it's nice to catch a lot of fish, but it's beautiful—just the atmosphere and the wilderness," opined Orville. "Everybody wants to catch big fish, of course, and you may some weeks catch a lot of fish, and other weeks it may be tougher. It all depends on the conditions that you have at the time. And each week is different than the next week and this is what we go by."

Hey, I'm not complaining. I had a great time and so did the sports from the United States—everybody said they'd go back in a heartbeat. The trip will go down as one of my best-ever fly fishing excursions. You know why? Awesome Lake is awesome—it's wilderness fishing personified! Despite the tough weather, and maybe because of it, I treasured each and every hook-up and took a lot of satisfaction in catching some fine trophies.

On the way home, over a beer in St. John's, Newfoundland, one of the locals and I got to talking. "In Labrador, you can have all four seasons in one day," he kidded. I could relate to this observation. We had wind, rain, sun, fog; the lake even came up over a foot during the course of one day. Everyone got wet, lots of times. The flags were washed hourly. The instability made for slow fishing and a long time between hook sets.

Fishing from a Gander River boat on Awesome Lake.

Orville Caddy with a mouse fly pattern.

Orville's favourite Labrador flies, mice and the baseball-sized lemmings that you needed both hands to pitch. I also caught fish on some of my favourite western Canadian flies: Chernobyl Ants and a Madame X. I just knew these western patterns would work. John Huff, Quebec fishing guide, had hinted as much on outings with him: the flies are different than what the local brook trout often see, and that's why they work. There was a selection of some 60-odd patterns in the lodge fly shop—that's right, 60 patterns, I counted them. Some of the best patterns during my trip were the Labrador Mouse, Jointed Lemming, Black Woolhead Sculpin, White Wulff, Muddler Minnow, Olive Woolly Bugger, Green Machine, Chernobyl Ant and Madame X.

It was great to share in the camaraderie of the experience with Orville—he never complained, not once. When fishing was slow, he was the first to suggest a change up, drawing on a huge selection from his many hand-tied flies. I caught fish on

I knew there were fish in Awesome Lake, lots of them, but the tough weather made fly casting a challenge and fly selection even more so because there was practically no insect activity during my stay— I saw only a few blue winged olives and one hatch of green drakes flying high one evening, no caddis flies and only one adult stonefly. Regardless, on one of my

Orville Caddy's fly box for brook trout.

A Twin Otter waiting at the remote Awesome Lake Lodge.

best days, I caught seven or eight brook trout 12–24 inches long, with two about 4 pounds. Three fish that were 5 pounds or better were taken at intervals, and all were well earned because sometimes you'd only get maybe one strike in an hour of fishing.

On my last night at Awesome Lake, I almost gave Tom Weaver of Maine a heart attack. I startled him on the patio as he watched the heavens, spellbound. We were both awed by a spectacular display of northern lights: an eerie fluorescent green band of light painted across the whole of an ink black sky, flaring along the edges—who cares how many brook trout were landed? When the Twin Otter roared over the lodge for the return trip to Goose Bay that last afternoon of our stay and the guides posed on the dock, I couldn't help but get a bit nostalgic. It was like leaving family behind.

If You Go

Awesome Lake Lodge went out of business for a few years, but it is now open again. A fishing travel package includes: ground transportation in Goose Bay, a charter flight to and from the lodge, guides (1:2), accommodations (2 persons per cabin) and home-cooked meals prepared by full-time cook. Look them up on the Newfoundland and Labrador Tourism website.

Yukon's Kathleen River: Top of the World Rainbows

"Now, was that exciting?" exclaimed my fishing guide, Thomas Staub, with that school-boy grin of his, bright blue eyes sparkling in the glow of the setting sun. We had just left the serpentine channel of Yukon's Kathleen River below Kathleen Lake, and I had taken a deep breath out of relief as much as exhilaration as he prepared to cut the motor, scant moments before the end of the day trip. Whew—talk about an adventure! From the time the jet boat hit the water early in the morning until the moment that marked the end of the trip, it was non-stop action. My fishing partner, Uwe Ammon, hailing all the way from Germany, likewise had a look on his face that belied both euphoria as well as some nervous tension.

Thomas had had to gun the 20-foot aluminum skiff—with the 40-horsepower Suzuki motor going at full bore—keeping to the outside bend as we returned to the launch site, always jockeying to stay in the deepest part of the shallow river channel and constantly on the lookout for snags, sweepers and shoals. The plume from the jet leg splayed behind the transom. Yes, it had been a white-knuckle ride back upriver to the launch site. In retrospect, it had been quite the day, fly fishing for rainbow trout on the Kathleen River; throw in a few Arctic grayling as an added bonus. I definitely had plans to celebrate the day's events with a cool Arctic Red beer when we returned to the Dalton Trail Lodge that evening—once I caught my breath, that is, and my heartbeat returned to normal.

The Kathleen River arises in Kluane National Park, at the feet of the mighty St. Elias Mountains, Canada's Himalayas. I'd finally had the opportunity to fish for rainbow trout on the Kathleen River after an aborted trip on an earlier visit to Yukon—rare, because this is Canada's northernmost population of rainbow trout. There

Thomas Staub jet boating on the Kathleen River.

are other reports of rainbow trout in only the East Aishihik River and Frederick Lake in Yukon. They're distinct populations to say the least, having probably crossed over the Continental Divide from Alaska during the last Ice Age. All rainbow trout caught must be released, and only single-pointed barbless hooks are permitted. The Kathleen is a large river, too deep to ford in most places; it can only be fished effectively with a jet boat. There are impassable falls in its lower reaches, and it's a one-way trip downstream with a raft or canoe. Don't even think about trying it without a competent fishing guide in a jet boat unless you have a death wish or are prepared for a long walk home.

In addition to abundant rainbow trout, the Kathleen River has a population of Arctic grayling; seasonally, kokanee, lake trout and lake whitefish also frequent its waters.

It's a fly fisherman's dream with lots of long, deep runs and many fine pools along the main stem of the river, which is interspersed with a series of "lakes" that add to the diversity of the experience. In most places you don't have to worry about your back cast hanging up on any tree branches, and the substrate is kind on your feet; no need to worry about slippery boulders and heavy cobble.

According to the owners of the Dalton Trail Lodge (see page 195), the best time to fish for rainbows is in June and August, although July and September are both good bets. The rainbows are no slouches and can reach up to 24 inches. I caught some in the 20- to 22-inch range and several above 15 inches. While fishing for Arctic grayling was slow on this particular trip, I did manage to take several nice ones. We missed out on large Arctic

The waters are crystal clear in the Kathleen River.

A rainbow trout from the Kathleen River.

grayling—other guys caught three that reached 18.5 inches the week prior to my trip—which were tight lipped, possibly because the river was flowing high.

The majesty of the area and its solitude are captivating—you can't help but feel humbled in this vast, unspoiled wilderness with the snow-capped St. Elias Mountains towering to the west, brooding amid the clouds high above the boreal forest. Swallows darted just above the deck, picking off a meagre hatch of mayflies. Bald eagles graced the sky, on an easy glide over their vast domain. A steady breeze from the southwest kept the mosquitoes at bay in this dry Yukon spring. In fact, I don't think that I got even one bite.

The prospect of my catching rainbow trout in their northernmost location in Canada was fairly palpable as Thomas Staub readied the jet boat. I'd missed out the first

time around a few years earlier when the Kathleen River was in flood. I had a feeling that this time I'd get even. It was a cool spring day: the ambient temperature ranged from 12 to 15° C, while the water temperature stayed steady at 8° C throughout the day, with overcast skies and sunny breaks in the afternoon. The fishing for Arctic grayling was slow, although I did manage to land several of those finny gems, but for rainbows it was red hot, and did they battle.

The Kathleen River is best fished for rainbows with a sink tip fly line and a short leader—no more than 3 feet long—if the flows are high. Pitch the streamer to the far side of the bank, let it sink in a dead drift—slowly strip, strip, strip—and stay tuned for a strike. Watch for bites as the fly reaches its downstream swing in particular. At the tail end of the dead drift, hold the streamer tight in the current, twitching it occasionally to entice a strike from passive trout. Active trout will grab it at any time. I had one attack the streamer not once, not twice, but three times before it was finally hooked—the price to pay for long, trailing marabou—and it porpoised several times. What a joy to fish for forgiving rainbows! Or, troll a streamer in the "lakes" that are interspersed between long stretches of the Kathleen River where it widens and the current becomes a bit slack. A fast troll worked best with short lines held at right angles to the boat. You had to power strip the whole time to entice strikes when trolling. The rainbows are suckers for this technique. It never failed.

A blue streamer (damselfly) and a cone-head purple Woolly Bugger were deadly on the rainbows. A Royal Wulff was the best dry fly for Arctic grayling, although I did get a few on the Woolly Bugger.

Other rainbow standbys include the Green Bug and the bead head wire worm Peacock fly pattern.

Most of the rainbows were chromers, like a steelhead in appearance. They were scrappy and hard fighters. They jumped more often and fought as hard as lower Bow River rainbows, and their similarities became apparent. Believe me: rainbows on the Bow River know how to tango, but the Kathleen River population doesn't play second fiddle to those trout.

If You Go

Visit the Department of Tourism and Culture website to request a vacation guide, or go to the Travel Yukon website.

The Kathleen River is the top stream for rainbows in Yukon.

The main lodge at Dalton Trail Lodge.

Dalton Trail Lodge, Yukon: Something for Everyone

I don't know of many fishing lodges North of 60 that have a paved road running right to their doorstep or a lounge and dining room with international cuisine that would rival those found in Canadian cities to the south. Forget the diet—you're not going to lose any weight at this place! How does this menu sound? Appetizer: pork tenderloin satay with peanut sauce. A salad buffet. Main course: baked chicken breasts in a light tomato sauce, with rice pilaf and leeks au gratin. Dessert: rhubarb strudel. And a full bar service with a large selection of wines. Then there are rooms with a full bath in a cedar-log building and cozy, upscale lakeside cabins. No wall tents, cans of pork and beans or outdoor

toilets in this fish camp! It's a place where you're made to feel welcome and at home by co-owners Hardy and Trix Ruff and their partners, where you're on a first-name basis upon arrival. Small wonder that the National Geographic *Traveler* magazine granted three stars to Dalton Trail Lodge, the highest designation awarded by this publication.

Yes, Dalton Trail Lodge is a first-class fishing lodge. The lodge trophies stand testament to the fabulous fishing opportunities in the area. If you get tired of fishing—which is hard to imagine—you could even try your hand at panning for gold. Dalton Trail Lodge has its own gold claim, and clients do find gold, especially when the local rivers are down. If you're interested in photography, wildlife abounds throughout

A lake trout taken by the author on a fly rod in Dezadeash Lake.

the area—moose, black and grizzly bears, mountain goats, Dall sheep, bald eagles, etc. There were five bears on the highway from Haines Junction to Dalton Trail Lodge the day I arrived on the first trip I made to this lodge—one grizzly and four black bears. I've been to the lodge six times and seen lots of wildlife on all the trips, including a grizzly up close on my second last trip. You can take ATV tours, go horseback riding, river rafting, mountain biking, hiking or canoeing.

The lodge is situated on the shore of Dezadeash Lake on the eastern border of Kluane National Park, which is absolutely awesome; there's nothing else quite like it in Canada. The towering St. Elias Mountains form a spectacular backdrop west of Dalton Trail Lodge, with their snow-capped peaks rising like daggers towards sparkling blue skies.

Dezadeash Lake is a fisherman's paradise, with lake trout, northern pike, Arctic grayling, lake whitefish and burbot. The area is known as the "Land of Big Fish" for good reason. The lake is warm and relatively shallow; consequently, growth rates of fish are much better than in typical lakes in Yukon, which tend to be deep and cold and not nearly as productive for fish. Lake trout top out at 40 pounds, and northern pike go up to 30 pounds. It is a big, sometimes windswept lake—not for sissies!

Special fishing regulations apply at Dezadeash Lake, which is being managed as a "Special Management Water" and is restricted to single-pointed, barbless hooks. Special catch limits apply for lake trout, Arctic grayling and northern pike, and you must have a Yukon fishing licence.

Myles Radford with a pike from Six Mile.

If you get tired of fishing Dezadeash Lake, Dalton Trail Lodge offers many trips to nearby lakes and rivers. A must-do trip is on the Kathleen River, which has one of only a few populations of rainbow trout found in Yukon, in addition to Arctic grayling, kokanee and lake trout (see page 191). Aishihik Lake is another prime destination that features a stay in a backcountry cabin, where one of the tourists at the lodge caught a 47-pound lake trout during my first visit. The Tatshenshini River for king (Chinook), sockeye and coho salmon also comes highly rated and is best fished during the last two weeks of July for salmon. I've enjoyed fly fishing for Dolly Varden in Stella Lake, with a local bald eagle as a spectator during one trip, while my son, Myles, and I experienced a close brush with a grizzly on another occasion. I've fly fished for pike at Six Mile after a heart-stopping quad ride through the bush from the doorstep of Dalton Trail Lodge. There are many other lakes and streams in the area featuring day trips— about 20 in all, so you're not going to get bored!

A Dolly Varden from Stella Lake.

Playing a lake trout in Dezadeash Lake.

Dalton Trail Lodge offers a wide range of fishing packages, meals and accommodations. Even if you didn't go fishing, I'm sure that you would enjoy yourself. It has been booked full during a couple of my visits, and some guests book in for two to three weeks at a time. The lodge opens on the Victoria Day weekend in May and closes the last week in September. Fishing guides can be provided depending on what kind of package you're interested in. However, after a one-day, break-in session on Dezadeash Lake, most anglers would be able to look after themselves, weather permitting.

One other thing I like about the lodge is that you can bring your catch home at the end of the day and one of the chefs will prepare all or part of it for you as a fish appetizer, which is a nice touch—a fishing trip just isn't complete without a meal or two of fresh fish. Another hook is that you can fly fish for a variety of fish from the lodge during one trip—lake trout, Arctic grayling, Dolly Varden, northern pike and rainbow trout, plus salmon at certain times of the year—all in one stay in a variety of action-packed adventures.

If You Go

Dalton Trail Lodge is located on Dezadeash Lake, directly bordering Kluane National Park south of Haines Junction, Yukon, a short distance from the Haines Road. The sun shines 24 hours a day in summer, and this is truly the Land of the Midnight Sun. Contact the lodge for further information and to make a reservation.

Northwest Territories Grayling Paradise

The Northwest Territories (NWT) has set the bar for record Arctic grayling, so it should be top on your bucket list if you're a fly fishing enthusiast. It holds the world record of 5 pounds, 15 ounces, for an Arctic grayling taken in the Katseyedie River by Jeanne Bransen on August 16, 1967. This outstanding record may never be broken, but it has been challenged a few times in recent years, so you never know.

Grayling are distributed across Alaska, Yukon, the NWT and Nunavut, as well as northern British Columbia, Alberta, Saskatchewan and Manitoba, but not in the islands of the Canadian Arctic Archipelago. They can be found in both lakes and streams throughout the north, where they'll usually readily take a fly, but not

always. I don't think there is a species of fish on earth that's more of a delight to catch by fly fishing than an Arctic grayling. They'll also often take small spinners and spoons, so spin casters can share in the action; grayling are a treat to catch on lightweight spinning gear, but that's another story.

I've fished for grayling in Alberta and Saskatchewan, as well as in Yukon and the NWT, with both of these territories boasting some tremendous grayling fishing. The NWT has set the bar for Canadian trophy grayling, however, with Jeanne Bransen's All-Tackle IGFA World Record. I've been fortunate to have fly fished for grayling on the NWT's storied Stark River and Sulky River.

I'd opt for a 4- to 6-weight fly rod, preferably with a mid-flex, which is suitable for a wide range of casting conditions and

A dark colour phase of Arctic grayling from the Sulky River, NWT.

styles that an itinerant angler would likely experience in the NWT. I'd also match the line weight with the rod, not overload it, because you usually don't need to make long casts. However, a fly casting trick is to use a fly line size that's rated one size larger than the rod weight to punch streamers, in particular, that much farther, especially when wind is expected to be an issue. I'd use a floating line (weight forward), packing a fast sink tip as a backup, just in case you run into some heavy water. If you're fishing on either the Stark River, for example out of Frontier Fishing Lodge on Great Slave Lake, or the Sulky, which is a fly-out from Plummer's Arctic Lodges' Great Bear Lake Lodge, you'll likely be okay with just a floating line. A sink tip line would come in handy on lakes such as Great Bear and Great Slave,

both of which have lots of inshore grayling. A mid-arbour reel with about 50 yards of Dacron backing is adequate. You won't need a large-arbour reel for grayling.

You should use a 9-foot, tapered leader with a 3-foot, 3X tippet for grayling. In my experience, it isn't necessary to use fluoro-carbon leaders; nylon is adequate. Most streams and lakes in Canada's north drain at least some muskeg, which releases tan-nins and lignins that tend to taint the water a slight brownish colour, rendering fluorocarbon leaders unnecessary.

If there's an insect hatch underway, you obviously want to try to match the hatch. There's a relative paucity of aquatic insect variety in the north, but black flies, small mayflies and caddis flies are present, as well as chironomids in lakes. Small dry

Fly fishing for grayling on the Stark River, NWT.

Attractor patterns and dry flies suitable for Arctic grayling.

flies such as Black Gnats, Elk Hair Caddis, Goddard Caddis, Royal Wulff and Red or Orange Humpys are all good producers.

If there's no active hatch, which is often the situation, you should start off by using attractor patterns such as the Madame X, Turk's Tarantula, Stimulators and Chernobyl Ant patterns. Attractor patterns are also called searching flies (for a good reason) because they'll help you find active fish to get some action. These often gaudy patterns imitate large stoneflies and terrestrial insects, nothing in particular, but the sort of invertebrates that catch the attention of grayling on the feed. They're easy to see and, in the often clear waters in the Precambrian shield where muskeg is lacking, can be dynamite on grayling.

Often, if you're fishing for grayling in a lake and the wind is calm, the fish will be rising all along the shoreline, so sight casting can be a real treat. However, if a wind picks up, the rise will suddenly fall off and you'll have to switch to a streamer. This is where a sink tip line comes in handy to get the fly down into their feeding zone. If I'm targeting larger grayling in either lakes or streams and rivers, I go with streamers that imitate bait fish and large aquatic invertebrates such as leaches, a favourite food of virtually all salmonids. My favourite streamers are earth coloured (e.g., black, brown and olive) Woolly Buggers, with cone heads for streams and rivers. Muddler Minnows, which imitate sculpins, are also good choices because sculpins are one of the more abundant bait fish in the north.

If there isn't a hatch underway and streamers don't seem to be producing,

A Stark River, NWT, Arctic grayling.

then try using a bead head Prince Nymph or Gold Ribbed Hare's Ear searching nymph in streams and rivers, or a wet black fly. Nymphs can actually be red-hot in both lakes and streams and are sometimes the fallback option that produce some great fishing, especially during inclement weather.

Now that you're armed with knowledge regarding fly fishing techniques, why don't you make some plans to partake in an excursion for Arctic grayling in the NWT? You won't be disappointed. There are numerous lakes and streams in the NWT that are teeming with grayling, so don't put off your plans to enjoy fishing for Canada's quintessential sport fish. And who knows, you might just set a new world record in the process.

If You Go

Fishing for grayling is outstanding on the Stark River, which is located near Frontier Fishing Lodge on Great Slave Lake.

Likewise, excellent fly fishing for grayling can be enjoyed on a fly-out to the Sulky River from Plummer's Arctic Lodge on Great Bear Lake. Plummer's has been hosting an annual fly fishing week each August out of Great Bear Lake since 2006, which is a good opportunity to share in the camaraderie of a fly fishing group.

B&J Fly Fishing Adventures: Arctic Char on Nunavut's Ekaluk River

There's something about fly fishing for Arctic char on the Ekaluk River on the Canadian tundra. You're far from all the trappings of civilization, maybe looking over your shoulder for wandering Barren Ground grizzly bears, thinking about a feast of caribou for dinner, and wondering whether you're going to set a new world record with your next cast. It's almost magical.

The Ekaluk River drains from Ferguson Lake into Wellington Bay in the Arctic Ocean on the Barren Grounds of the Arctic Archipelago on Victoria Island. During my trip, I could sense the spirits of Nunavut's Ekaluk River Inuit char hunters as I cast into the swiftly flowing waters,

trying to entice yet another Arctic char to hit my streamer. Lichen-encrusted boulders from long-abandoned caribou drives, food caches, tent dwellings and fox traps peppered the landscape near the river. It is obvious that the Inuit have left their mark on the landscape beside the famed char river. My guess is that Ekaluk River char have developed a "bank avoidance adaptive mechanism" over thousands of years because the Inuit would have speared them throughout history; any char that didn't avoid the shore could end up in a char cache.

I was on a dream trip at B&J Fly Fishing Adventures wilderness camp, which is owned by Bill and Jessie Lyall of Cambridge Bay, Nunavut. Bill's father, Ernie, wrote *An Arctic Man* (2001), a fascinating first-person account of Ernie's life as a Hudson Bay Company man and as

The Ekaluk River where it flows into Wellington Bay on the Arctic Ocean.

Inuit artifacts beside the Ekaluk River on the tundra.

Bill Lyall, owner of B&J Fly Fishing Adventures camp on the Ekaluk River.

a government official in the Canadian eastern arctic, a career that spanned 65 years from 1910 to 1975. Bill Lyall, one of the eldest Lyall boys, was president of Arctic Co-operative Ltd. in Cambridge Bay at the time of my trip in 2012. He attended school in Yellowknife and later enrolled in the Northern Alberta Institute of Technology in Edmonton. The camp is managed by Jack Elofsson of Calgary, a retired Swedish merchant mariner who is Bill's partner. Jack once quipped to me that "This place is holy," perhaps not truly comprehending the nature of his claim in the context of all the Inuit archeological artifacts.

It took me several years to pull off this once-in-a-lifetime fly fishing trip. There's a long waiting list for the relatively few openings because repeat clients have been the norm since it first opened for business in 2001; 2012 was an exception with some openings during the first week of a two-week late-August season. This was not my first experience fly fishing for Arctic char, having twice visited the storied Tree River (see page 211). I knew what kind of challenges I would likely face. Regardless, I still had a surreal time hooking and landing char in the Ekaluk River, one of Canada's most outstanding char fisheries. It's quite possible the next world-record char will be landed on its banks. Char fishing was the main attraction, but the many other facets to my arctic adventure, including the unique northern cuisine of bannock, char, muskox and caribou at the camp, made the trip a truly memorable experience. The camp on the Ekaluk River is rustic but comfortable and has electricity when the generator is on to provide power to the cabins, charge digital camera batteries and the like.

An Arctic char that taped 36 inches from the Ekaluk River.

The B&J Fly Fishing wilderness camp is rustic but comfortable.

A muskox bull skull on the harsh tundra near the Ekaluk River.

This place is for fly fishers only—spinning and bait casting gear are not permitted. Stay home if you're not up to walking several miles over the tundra each day, often fly fishing under weather conditions that would keep most anglers inside. The weather can be brutal, with gale force winds, fog, rain and numbing cold. On the other hand, it can also be warm and sunny—downright pleasant. And you rarely have to worry about getting snagged on your back cast because there are no trees on the tundra, only occasional shrubs.

A "tire run" is a classic football drill that hones a player's speed and agility—you've likely seen videos of it. Tires are laid out side by side, with each tire on the left a few inches ahead of the tire on the right in a zigzag pattern. There are at least 10 tires in this pattern. Players start at one end of the line and run down the line of tires while stepping left foot in the left tires and right foot in the right tires. That's more or less

what it's like to walk on the tundra. While the tundra looks like it's level from the air, it isn't. The vegetated landscape is pockmarked with shallow depressions. Throw in the occasional stretch of melting permafrost and you'll have a facsimile of what I'd call a "tundra walk." It can be exhausting at times. I would say I put in 15 kilometres (9 miles) a day of tundra walking, six days in a row during my stay at B&J Fly Fishing Adventures camp on the Ekaluk River. A word of advice: get in shape before you leave home, and pace yourself during your trip.

My roommate was Paul Lawson from Houston, Texas, who had been on many canoe trips to the Canadian north. Paul was a great guy, easy to get along with and a keen fly fisher who had fly fished all over North and South America. I also shared the camp with three other fly fishers, all from Calgary. Nine anglers were booked for the second and last week of the season. Paul and I would hit the sack at 9:00 PM (bone tired) and rise at 6:00 AM for an early breakfast before heading out for a day on the water.

The larger char had their way with the fly fishers in camp, often stripping 100–200 feet (or more) of line in a single run, pushing fly rods and reels to the limit. I broke my best rod in three places on day two of the trip! Fortunately, I'd packed a couple of spare rods, so I wasn't out of action very long. The trip was akin to playing in Carnegie Hall, but I was alone on the tundra when I beached my best char, which taped an even 36 inches.

The chrome-bodied beauty was but one of many fine char I would land during the course of my arctic adventure, scant yards from where I'd noticed Barren Ground grizzly bear tracks in the sand earlier in the trip. Grizzlies crossed the sea ice from the mainland onto Victoria Island around

Barren Ground grizzly bear tracks beside the Ekaluk River.

1987. There are no polar bears in the area, but muskoxen are quite common. The resident caribou on Victoria Island were to the north of our camp and don't venture south until later on in October, when the ocean freezes and they cross to the mainland.

The Ekaluk River was divided into various "beats," from the Home Pool near camp to the Rapids, where the river drains from

The author with an Arctic char on the Ekaluk River.

Rocky Run reach on the Ekaluk River, with the Arctic Ocean in the distance.

Ferguson Lake before it enters Wellington Bay in the Arctic Ocean. The Rapids are about a 4-kilometre (2.5-mile) walk from camp. Master fishing guide Jack Elofsson suggested that clients follow what is basically Atlantic salmon fly fishing protocol if they were on the same beat: spread out and fish downstream, take a couple of casts, then take two or three steps downstream. Repeat the process. If you hook a char, go back to the start of the beat so you don't hog the better lies. It's a simple formula. When I was fly fishing by myself, which was not uncommon, I'd chase the char much like I would fly fish for steelhead. Although the char run had started, they weren't everywhere; plus they were moving upstream, and you had to search them out.

I was rigged with an 8-weight fly rod with an intermediate sink tip line and 100 yards of Dacron backing on a large-arbour reel. You don't need a tapered leader; a few feet of 20-pound monofilament will work just fine.

There are a variety of fly patterns that will catch char: Deceivers, Zonkers and Woolly Buggers all preferably weighted. Pink was probably the best colour, followed by chartreuse. "Guide flies" are available for sale in camp.

When I fished the Ekaluk River in 2012, I saw only a handful of rising char, and it was impossible to see what they were feeding on, but it was likely some form of terrestrial insect. I asked Jack Elofsson about insect hatches and flies. He said, "There are no hatches of any kind on the river, and I have yet to find a bug under a rock. However, we catch fish on 'dries' all the time—big Bombers, greased up Muddlers, modified Hoppers and whatever. Also nymphs—big dark San Juan-type nymphs imitating the arctic mini-shrimp [a staple in the diet of char in the ocean]. The sea-run fish is actively feeding in the river—very aggressive, attacks most anything properly presented—and makes for an exciting fishery." Jack also said that some fly colours produce far better than others: "Presentation is the key to success. We use traditional Atlantic salmon patterns, Scandinavian tube flies, large streamers, huge dry flies or nymphs. Over the years, a handful of dynamite Ekaluk patterns have evolved. It shall be noted that we fish only for the fresh sea-run fish. We don't fish 'early season' for the ocean-bound post-spawners [the brightly coloured and photogenic fish one commonly sees on photos]."

Fish streamers using a classic Atlantic salmon across and down cast, mend the line to sink the streamer, twitch the line during a dead drift, and strip the fly slowly during the retrieve. Keep the tip of your fly rod pointed towards the streamer. It's that simple. A word of advice for those unfamiliar with char fishing: when a char strikes, you may think you've snagged the bottom, but don't be fooled. Set the hook hard, then give it a couple of extra tugs to make sure your hook is set, especially when fishing with a barbless hook, which is easily thrown. Use your reel's drag and the flex in your fly rod to slow a char's run. When it stops, pump your rod and reel in some line. Chase char, which can go up or downstream. It's amazing how fast they can accelerate in either direction or across stream; they'll go in several directions before you land one.

B&J Fly Fishing Adventures camp on the Ekaluk River is located about 72 kilometres (45 miles) northwest of Cambridge

Jack Elofsson fillets an Arctic char beside the Ekaluk River.

Bay. You'll take a float plane from Cambridge Bay to the camp, flying low over the tundra. The maximum number of clients is 12 fishermen per week. Bill Lyall's daughter, Fiona, ferried me from the airport to the float plane base on the Arctic Ocean, which is the take-off point to the camp. Bill's son Willy was a camp attendant. During my stay, Mike Mailey helped out with cooking and camp duties. Mike is a fishing guide with SouthBow Fly & Tackle Ltd. in Calgary. Both Mike and Jack Elofsson are fishing guides and will provide Arctic char fly fishing advice and instruction. However, you're on your own while on the water, unguided. The whole trip is quite an adventure that every serious fly fisher should have on his or her bucket list.

If You Go

Check out B&J Fly Fishing Adventures' website and Nunavut Tourism to plan your trip. The camp manager will provide a suggested equipment list. There are daily flights from Edmonton to Cambridge Bay on Canadian North and First Air, with a stopover in Yellowknife. Sport fishing licences can be obtained in camp. A word of warning: it is not uncommon for both charter and commercial flights to be delayed or cancelled in the Canadian arctic due to inclement weather.

Mike Mailey rings a triangle to signal dinner.

Nunavut's Tree River: The Ultimate Arctic Char

As an inveterate fly fishing junkie, I've travelled across Canada from coast to coast to coast sampling the fly fishing, especially those with a blue-ribbon reputation. Many of these hot spots, such as Alberta's Bow River and Ontario's Grand River, are easy to access. Others present more of a challenge, and a few, such as the Tree River in Nunavut, are challenging indeed.

There are several otherworldly Canadian fly fishing rivers, but perhaps the leader of the pack is the Tree River in Nunavut, largely because of its mystique and perhaps because the Tree River is home to the world-record Arctic char, a 32-pound, 9-ounce fish caught by Jeffrey Ward on July 30, 1981. The Tree River is iconic to char aficionados in Canada's fly fishing circles.

The Inuit name of the Tree River is Kugluktoaluk. Steven Curley of the Unikkaarvik Visitor Centre, Nunavut Tourism, provided a translation. He said the word kugluktuk means "moving water or rushing waters," and toaluk means "very much." Taken together, Kugluktoaluk means "major rushing waters."

A male (below) and female (above) Arctic char from the Tree River.

The Tree River Lodge, with the Tree River in the background.

The Tree River is a world giant in Arctic char circles and had been on my list of must-fish waters for a long time. When I stepped off a Turbo Otter onto its banks in August 2008, I felt as if I was walking onto hallowed ground. I had this surreal feeling that I was about to play in a championship game. And I guess I was because I was playing for all the marbles on what was the last trip of the year organized by Plummer's Arctic Lodges during their third-annual fly fishing week. All the hyperbole went out the window as I savoured the moment, and phrases such as "the trip of a lifetime" seemed rather inadequate under the circumstances.

Unquestionably, I found the Tree River to be one of the most challenging rivers I've ever tackled; plus, the cards were stacked against me from the start. On the first day of the trip, the Canadian party I was travelling with graciously agreed to let some foreign guests take the first of two Turbo Otter flights from Great Bear Lake to the Tree River Lodge, giving them a head start of several hours on the river and the best choice of pools on day one of our three-day trip, when (as it turned out) the weather was at its best.

As Sean Barfoot, then manager of Plummer's Tree River Lodge, explained during my stay, the lodge is located in one of the most remote spots in all of Canada relative to the nearest settlement—Kugluktuk (formerly Coppermine), 145 kilometres (90 miles) to the west. It's without the benefit of a nearby weather station, which means that the lodge manager has to keep a close eye on the weather, calling the shots for flights into the river when he judges that there's a clear window. So, when Shane Jonker, then overall operations manager at Plummer's Great Bear Lake Lodge—the departure point for the Tree River flights—huddled with the enthusiastic fly fishers after dinner to announce in hushed tones that the weather was clear enough to land at the Tree River the next day, I couldn't help but breathe a sigh of relief. Tomorrow would be the big day. It might not have happened had the weather not cleared. Arctic cold fronts can create immense fog banks near the lodge where the Tree River flows into Coronation Gulf, which makes float plane landings impossible. The flight from Great Bear Lake to the Tree River is about 300 kilometres (185 miles) and lasts two hours; float planes land right on the river downstream from the lodge, and clients are then ferried upstream by boat.

Larry Willet, my affable fishing guide at the Great Bear Lake Lodge, had told me the Tree River should be called the "Perseverance River." In a wake-up call on day one, I would find out why. Despite almost casting my arm off, I was rewarded with but a few strikes and char that quickly threw hooks in fast water. Forget the fact that the Tree River is at the edge of the continent and sees only scant fishing pressure during the open season. It's a turbo-charged white-water river, challenging to fly fish, with deep, swift pools and spotty pocket water, impossible to wade or ford in many reaches. A missed step could spell disaster in the foaming and treacherous current.

The Turbo Otter float plane waiting at Plummer's Great Bear Lake Lodge.

Fishing guide Trevor Nowak with the author, holding a fine lake trout from the Tree River.

When I eventually landed an Arctic char that taped 35.5 inches from Slippery Jack pool on day two of my trip, it was truly a life moment that I'll never forget: mission accomplished. I could have kissed my guide, Trevor Nowak, and cried for joy. I thanked my lucky stars for having Trevor as my Tree River mentor; he had been head guide at this lodge for the previous several seasons, prior to Sean Barfoot taking over. I took the char on a hand-tied olive Clouser streamer at 9:30 AM, when the ambient temperature and water temperature were an identical 10° C. But that wasn't all; I also took a lake trout that taped 40 inches with a 19-inch girth on a Mickey Finn the same day at 6:00 PM. These big lakers (a 26-pound specimen was recorded in 2008) and lake whitefish up to 8 pounds are frequently taken—trophy fish anywhere, but on the Tree River they tend to be overshadowed by the spectacular char.

A Tree River lake whitefish.

The author's Tree River fly box with various patterns of streamers, etc.

Guides tend to favour either unobtrusive fly patterns for char such as the Blue and Pink Rat wet flies or the gaudy Pixie's Revenge. I preferred natural patterns that imitated the local slimy sculpins, but I ran the gamut of patterns in my fly box. Prior to my trip, Plummer's Arctic Lodges guide Craig Blackie advised, "As in other systems, fresh fish are easy to catch, while fish that have been in the river awhile can become more difficult. Part of the issue relates to the conditions of the river. Early season sees the river high with snow melt, and by August, the river is typically low and clear. That being said, a good rain can blow out the river at any time of year. What this means for fishing is that you must adjust your flies and tactics accordingly." Craig added: "A general rule of thumb is 8- to 10-weight rods with heavy, 12- to 15-foot sink-tips and large streamers or Spey flies. Productive patterns

include Zonkers, Clouser Minnows, Lefty's Deceivers, Mickey Finns, Spey flies such as GPs and popsicles. This system applies when the fish are active. When fishing gets tough, I prefer to switch to a floating line and dead drift smaller versions of these streamers under a strike indicator. As for sizes, when the water is high, I use sizes 2–2/0 and when the water is low, I'll scale it down to sizes 4–10. It's important to weight the flies with dumbell eyes, cone heads, etc."

Craig Blackie's Tree River Arctic char fly.

Despite the tough fishing conditions, all eight fly fishers in my party landed at least one char during our trip, while some were rewarded with several nice fish. Although I had done a lot of research on how to catch char and what fly patterns were producers, I must admit to having had second thoughts about catching even one at times. The Tree River can be a heartbreaker, and for those who've never walked its banks, my advice is to go well prepared to fish long and hard, and be ever positive. Just catching an Arctic char on the Tree River can be a major accomplishment, especially late in the season when they've seen just about every lure on the market go by, and they are gearing up to spawn and are therefore off the feed—virtually all fish landed at this time of the year have empty stomachs, according the guides.

The Tree River might better be called the "River of Giant Fish," and after talking to local fishing guides and scientists, I think I might know why it's such a superlative river. Because the river is so swift and turbulent, its finny denizens have evolved into some of the toughest salmonids in the world. Tree River char are notable for lessened genetic variability, and the guides are of the opinion that natural selection has favoured only the strongest of char in this most turbulent of arctic rivers—the Tree River features numerous thunderous falls, rapids and chutes. There's intense competition for spawning habitat because of impassable waterfalls that are a barrier to

Falls on the turbulent Tree River.

The Barren Grounds to the west of the Tree River Lodge.

upstream movement not far above the Presidential Pool. Only the lower 10 kilometres (6 miles) of the Tree River are accessible to the char, which can be seen slowly edging their way upriver.

The Tree River valley is verdant compared to the rather desolate surrounding Barren Grounds and abounds with wildlife. I noticed Barren Ground grizzly bear scats on the trail to the third falls and spotted a lone white wolf by the Presidential Pool. I also watched a peregrine falcon scoop a willow ptarmigan from the air, followed by ear-piercing screeches as it carried its quarry to a nearby perch. There were numerous coveys of willow ptarmigan that graced the trails on either side of the river, and it was possible to approach within a few feet of the various flocks. Moose and Barren Ground caribou are often sighted, as well as muskoxen, near the lodge. Golden and bald eagles graced the often leaden skies during my trip, while arctic ground squirrels (sik-siks) darted about the grounds of the lodge, keeping an ever-watchful eye out for avian predators.

What a trip it was—one of the pinnacles of my life. Just getting to this fabled river in search of the Holy Grail of Arctic fly fishing legends, the world-renowned Tree River's Arctic char was a wonderful experience among a host of famous Canadian fly fishing waters.

An Inuit rock drawing near the Tree River.

If You Go

Plummer's Lodge Contact Information: For details regarding the upcoming annual fly fishing weeks at Great Bear Lodge, which features a side trip to the Tree River Lodge, or custom trips exclusive to the Tree River, check out Plummer's Arctic Lodge's website. Charter flights are available from Kugluktuk to the Tree River Lodge for exclusive expeditions on the Tree River.

Fishing Regulations: Clients can fly fish for Arctic char at any time during the open season on the Tree River. Although the department of Fisheries and Oceans permits an annual harvest of 350 fish from the Tree River per season, Plummer's Arctic Lodges restricts the take to just 32, which are served up as fare in the lodge kitchen—and only one fish per party. Otherwise, fishing is strictly catch-and-release. To minimize hooking injuries, barbless hooks are mandatory.

Sunset over the Tree River.

Glossary of Fly Fishing Terms

attractor (search) pattern: a large, conspicuous fly that floats high on the water; used to locate actively feeding fish, especially when fishing large streams when no obvious hatch is in progress

back water: quiet water associated with an old stream channel

Belgian cast: a power cast used to pitch large streamers, usually employed when fishing with a sink tip line; rather than pausing on the back cast, the angler keeps the rod in motion and rotates the line forward, casting ahead to propel a fly toward a target

bitch fly: a hand tied, no-name fly pattern that fancies the person who tied it

blind casting: the opposite of sight casting, where the angler does not see a fish and is casting over a grid in search of his quarry in promising holding water

chop cast: a short cast, usually made into the wind, featuring a shortened back cast and a powerful forward stroke to change the trajectory, throwing hard and tight; used to overcome the wind by lowering the angle of the fly rod just prior to releasing the line

dance (or skate) a fly: to make a dry fly move erratically by twitching the end of a fly rod

dog a lure: to pursue a lure as though on a scent trail (i.e., a fish will chase a lure much like a dog would chase something, often moving from side to side)

double haul cast: includes the single haul (the downward pull of line off a reel) on the back cast plus an additional haul on the forward cast; used to increase line speed

and casting distance when false casting; strip line while you are making a back cast, and feed line to the rod; down is for speed; up is for feeding line

drag-free drift: when a fly is drifting at the same speed as the current so it looks natural

dry fly: a fly pattern that floats on the surface of the water

emerger: a unique fly pattern that imitates the metamorphic stage between a larval and adult insect as it leaves the water; fished on the surface during a hatch

false cast: backward/forward straight-line cast(s) usually employed to shake water off a dry fly and dry it off

fly dressing: floatants designed to waterproof dry flies in the form of liquids, aerosol or pump-type sprays, pastes, etc., to help them float high on the water

freestone river/stream: a river/stream with no dams or diversions

frog water: quiet water adjacent to a stream bank (usually with a foam line) often near the head of a pool (in BC where migrating salmon tend to rest) or back water

guide fly: a "secret" fly pattern that fly fishing guides generally use only as a last resort when all the other patterns fail to entice a strike

high stick the rod/line: a technique most commonly used to finesse a fly over promising but tricky pocket water by holding the rod tip high in the air and dappling the fly on the surface of the water in a downstream direction

holding water: area associated with deep runs, the tail-out of pools, seams between pools and runs, etc., where fish find their comfort zone

hook set: the moment after a fish strikes when an angler sets the hook in its jaw

hook-up: follows a hook set when the fish is firmly hooked on the end of a line

horse a fish: to put more pressure on your fly line than necessary; don't do it, or the tippet, which is the weakest part of the line, will usually snap

invertebrate drift: a diurnal phenomena characterized by the emergence of aquatic insects from under rocks, gravel and boulders during the night, which then become dislodged and float downstream in the current; a phenomena which lessens during daylight hours

land a fish: to capture a fish in a landing net or fish cradle, sometimes by "banking" it (i.e., beaching it on a stream bank)

leader shy: pertains to fish that have exceptional vision and can detect ordinary monofilament leader, in which case a fluorocarbon leader that's virtually invisible is necessary

lining a fish: occurs when a colourful fly line is cast over top of trout that have exceptional vision, which will alarm them—in fly angling parlance, "put them down"—and they will not take a fly

load the rod: involves making a short cast and then using the surface tension on the water to create some drag so that when you lift your line out, the energy is transferred to the rod, which springs back and can then be put into the forward cast to make it easier to get a longer cast; also known as bending the rod; creates the forward and backward motion of the fly line

match the hatch: a saying among fly anglers that means using a dry fly that closely imitates insects that are actively hatching and flying over the water

mend the line: essential when fishing a trout stream in order to get a drag-free, natural drift; accomplished by lifting the line out of the water and looping it in an upstream direction when fishing with a dry fly; done anytime the fly line or leader starts to drift faster than the fly; if you're fishing a nymph or streamer, a downstream mend will sink the fly to "swim" it parallel to the stream bank; it's often necessary to make a number of mends in succession to achieve the desired effect throughout the drift

nymph (n.): a fly that imitates a larval insect, fished underwater, usually weighted with a bead head to sink it, which does not have any hackles on the thorax

nymph a fly: use a strike indicator above your fly (i.e., nymph or wet fly) with a lead split shot sinker about 18 inches above it that's heavy enough to sink it; try to fish it in a dead drift so it floats at the same speed as the current; as your line moves downstream, you can extend your run by feeding slack line into the drift

play a fish: once a fish is hooked, job one is to keep it on the line and try to ensure it doesn't throw the hook; keep a tight line by extending the rod high after bringing it under control by handling the fly line, not immediately taking it to reel unless it's a pike; once it's brought to reel, use the drag feature on the fly reel to slow its runs and don't try to land it until it is tired

pocket water: a hole or depression in a stream bottom created by a boulder

pool: still water in a river or stream

porpoise a fly: imitate the action of a porpoise by gently lifting and lowering your rod tip to make a fly rise and fall in the water to attract the attention of a fish

reach cast: a straight-line cast followed immediately by an upstream mend once the fly lands so it floats in a drag-free drift

riffle water: moving water, often on the edge of a seam

roll cast: after stripping some fly line at your feet, quickly rotate your wrist and cast forward, eliminating a back cast; the rod flex will pick up the slack line and propel it forward; used where vegetation is immediately behind the angler and/or where other obstacles are nearby

shooting head: multi-tip fly lines of varying weights and tapers recommended for steelhead fishing, particularly in BC, that are normally attached to a floating line to stretch casting distances; cast the line in the normal manner, and the shooting head will pull the fly line to enable a longer cast with less effort, with practice

sidearm cast: cast sideways to change the trajectory of the cast; use a power cast to get below the worst wind when casting into the wind or to maneuver a fly into a tight spot near a cliff on a stream bank

sight casting: casting towards a fish that is visible with the idea of presenting the fly just in front of the fish or on top of where its snout should be

slack-line cast: used to reach fish lying downstream of the angler; start by holding the rod tip low once the fly lands with a straight-line cast, then wiggle the line once it lands so that the fly floats in a drag-free drift as the line plays out

split shot: a small lead pellet used to sink a fly; split shots feature a grove that can be squeezed over a monofilament line for this purpose

sport: another word for a fellow fly angler

stack (mend) cast: helpful for streamer and nymph fishing by transferring slack line from a point near the rod to a point near the fly to sink it quickly; cast the fly beyond the target, and once it lands, pick the rod up into the position to start a roll cast; next, make a short, sharp roll cast directed low and at the location the fly landed; additional stack mends can be made successively to sink the fly even deeper

straight-line cast: used to deliver a fly by casting the line in a straight direction towards a target; start by stripping some line, and lay it at your feet or hold it in your hand; make a high back cast; bring the fly rod forward, accelerating, and throw a forward loop keeping the tip of your rod in a horizontal plane; let your line go when your rod tip is straight out in front of you and the tip is almost horizontal. Use only enough power to lay the line out straight; don't overpower your forward cast or the line will fall in a pile at your feet. You may have to make a few false casts to load the rod with enough line to reach your target; for large flies (e.g., streamers), use the water to load the fly rod rather than using false casts; use short strokes for short casts and long strokes for long casts; keep slack line to a minimum; don't use any more line than necessary to reach your target

streamer: a fly (often weighted) that sinks and imitates either minnows, leaches or other aquatic invertebrates

strike indicator: a small float attached to a leader above a fly that floats along the surface as your fly drifts in the current; the indicator will sink or move laterally if a fish strikes

strike zone: conditions where timing is such that there's a higher than normal probability of catching fish, often related to weather and barometric conditions (cold fronts, windy days, bright sunlight, high pressure systems and fluctuating water levels all seem to put fish off feeding), and/or the distance a fish will move to take a fly

strip the line: a strategy used when fishing with streamers; jerk the fly line towards you in short strips to entice hook-ups; to power strip the line when trolling with streamers, pull it hard in an upwards motion from time to time to catch the attention of active fish

swim a fly: involves a downstream mend when fishing with a streamer to both sink the fly and move it a little bit faster than the speed of a current

tail-out water: the slow-moving, shallow water at the bottom of a pool

tail water: rivers downstream of dams

troll: a fishing method where a fishing line is drawn through the water behind a boat, usually at a slow speed

wet fly: a fly that sinks and is meant to be fished under water

work the line: when fly fishing, handling a fly line is a must; always point the tip of the rod towards the fly; elevate the rod to keep a wet fly off the bottom; "porpoise" streamers in the water to attract the attention of fish; mend the line as often as necessary; hold the fly line between a couple of fingers to detect subtle strikes, especially when fishing with nymphs and streamers; let out and reel in line; etc.

yard on the line (or rod): to pull excessively on a hooked fish, which often causes the tippet to break and in extreme cases, even the rod tip

Notes on Sources and Further Reading

Online sources are cited in the text. Some of the following books might appear dated; they are, however, the most recent publications.

Danks, H.V. and Dowes, J.A. *Insects of the Yukon*. Biological Survey of Canada Mono graph series No. 2, Published by the BIOLOGICAL SURVEY OF CANADA (TERRESTRIAL ARTHROPODS), 1997.

Hanks, Chris. *Fly Fishing in the Northwest Territories in Canada*. Frank Amato Publisher. Portland, 1996.

Knopp, Malcom and Cormier, Robert. *Mayflies—An Angler's Study of Trout Water Ephemeroptera*. Greycliff Publishing Company, 1997.

Kreh, Lefty. *Lefty Kreh's Ultimate Guide to Fly Fishing—Everything Anglers Need to Know by the World's Foremost Fly-Fishing Expert*. Hardcover Publisher, 2003.

Lyall, Ernie. *An Arctic Man*. Formac Publishing Company Limited. Halifax, Nova Scotia, 2001.

Martin, Ian and Rutherford (Martin), Jane E. *Fly Fishing the Grand River: The Angler's Vest Pocket Guide*, 1995.

McPhail, J.D. and Lindsay, C.C. *Freshwater Fishes of Northwestern Canada and Alaska*. Bulletin 173. Fisheries Research Board of Canada, 1970.

Nelson, Joseph S. and Paetz, Martin J. *The Fishes of Alberta*. The University of Alberta and Calgary Press, 2nd Edition, 1992.

Radford, Duane S. and Shickler, Ross H. *Fishing Northern Canada For Lake Trout, Grayling and Arctic Char*. North Country Press, 2015.

Scott, W.B. and Crossman, E.J. *Freshwater Fishes of Canada*. Bulletin 184 Fisheries. Research Board of Canada, Ottawa, 1973.

Shickler, Ross H. and Eveland, Edward M. *Lake Trout—North America's Greatest Game Fish*. The Derrydale Press. Lanham and New York, 2001.

Soucie, Gary. *Soucie's Field Guide of Fishing Facts*. Fireside (Reprint Edition), 2008.

Walker, Jordan. *Status of the Arctic grayling (*Thymallus arcticus*) in Alberta* Alberta Wildlife Status Report No. 57, 2005.

Yukon Freshwater Fishes: Yukon Wild. Published by the Government of Yukon, 2009.

About the Author

Duane is a native of Bellevue, Alberta and currently lives in Edmonton, Alberta. He is a national award-winning writer and photographer whose articles and photographs have appeared in many outdoor publications and newspapers in Canada and the United States. He authored over 750 magazine articles and three award winning books: *Fish & Wild Game Recipes* (2006), *Conservation Pride and Passion: the Alberta Fish and Game Association 1908–2008* (2008), which he co-authored with Don Meredith, and *The Cowboy Way* (2014). He also co-edited a book with Ross H. Shickler, *Fishing Northern Canada for Lake Trout, Grayling and Arctic Char* (2015). Duane is the primary author of *The Canadian Cowboy Cookbook* (2015), which he co-authored with Jean Paré and G. Lepine.

Duane is the (former) North County and Alberta North field editor for *The Canadian Fly Fisher* magazine and has fished throughout much of Canada. He is a past president of the Outdoor Writers of Canada and served on their Board of Directors for eight years. He is a member of Trout Unlimited Canada, the Alberta Fish & Game Association, as well as a former director and vice president of the Edmonton Trout Fishing Club. Duane retired as the director of Alberta's fisheries management branch. He worked as a regional director, regional fisheries biologist and fishery scientist for Alberta's Fish and Wildlife Division. He is certified as a Fisheries Scientist by the American Fisheries Society. He represents Alberta on the National Recreational Fishery Awards Committee and is vice chairman of this committee. He is an honourary member of the Great Plains Fishery Workers Association. He was bestowed an Alberta Order of the Bighorn Award as a member of the Bow Habitat Station Core Committee in 1998, Alberta's foremost conservation award.